The Making of Artistic Typefaces

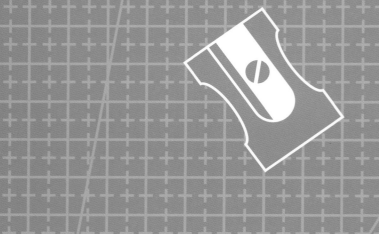

The Making of Artistic Typefaces

© 2016 SendPoints Publishing Co., Ltd.

SendPoints

EDITED & PUBLISHED BY SendPoints Publishing Co., Ltd.
PUBLISHER: Lin Gengli
PUBLISHING DIRECTOR: Lin Shijian
CHIEF EDITOR: Lin Shijian
EXECUTIVE EDITOR: Yan Guiling
ART DIRECTOR: He Wanling
EXECUTIVE ART EDITOR: Ho Waikin
PROOFREADING: Ellen Christensen, Yan Guiling

REGISTERED ADDRESS: Room 15A Block 9 Tsui Chuk Garden, Wong Tai Sin, Kowloon, Hong Kong
TEL: +852-35832323 / **FAX:** +852-35832448
OFFICE ADDRESS: 7F, 9th Anning Street, Jinsha Zhou, Baiyun District, Guangzhou, China
TEL: +86-20-89095121 / **FAX:** +86-20-89095206
BEIJING OFFICE: Room 107, Floor 1, Xiyingfang Alley, Ande Road, Dongcheng District, Beijing, China
TEL: +86-10-84139071 / **FAX:** +86-10-84139071
SHANGHAI OFFICE: Room 307, Building 1, Hong Qiang Creative, Zhabei District, Shanghai, China
TEL: +86-21-63523469 / **FAX:** +86-21-63523469

SALES MANAGER: Sissi
TEL: +86-20-81007895
EMAIL: overseas01@sendpoints.cn
WEBSITE: www.sendpoints.cn / www.spbooks.cn

ISBN 978-988-14703-7-9

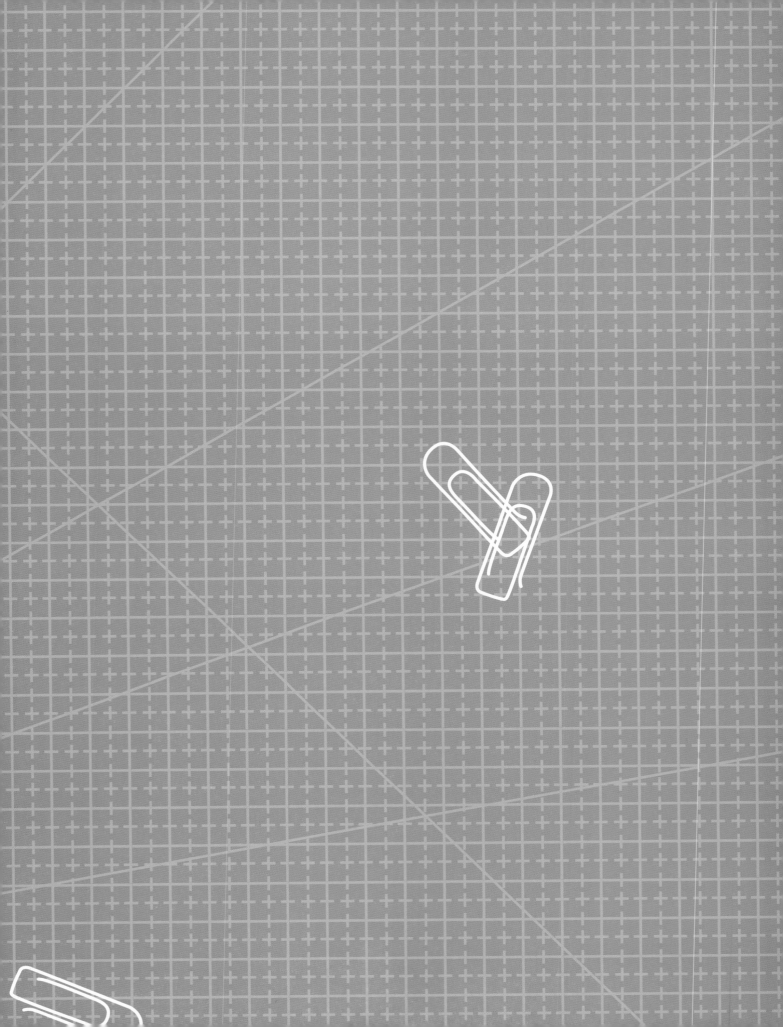

The Love Affair with Handcrafted Artistic Type

Camilo Rojas
Designer, Art Director & Founder @ CR-eate Studio, USA

When was the last time you picked up a pen to write a letter to someone? Or the last time you received a letter from someone in the mailbox? It's hard to remember. But if we look back we will revive the love affair with and idea coming to life through someone's handwriting. Handwritten letters will always feel more personal than typed letters and the same applies to typography as an art form.

Yet, the beauty of starting a project by hand is vanishing due to the strong digitalization and uniformity of the design profession. There is no doubt that recent technological advancements are outstanding and should be embraced and integrated into design, but the importance of handcrafting is not to be overlooked.

The handcrafting of typography is an extensive task that goes beyond making a pretty typeface. Handcrafting is about developing a concept that creates a meaningful impact, that is meant to be functional and designed to perfection. Unfortunately the quantity of typefaces available has created a uniformity in design. This lack of innovation has pushed many designers to explore other facets of typography. They have ventured once again into the world away from the computer and are exploring a more tactile and personal aesthetic, one which can take a critical view of a variety of social and cultural issues.

The importance of handcrafted artistic type has allowed the portal of graphic design as art to open in the art world. This window has restored the purpose of handcrafted artistic typefaces in design and art to be used in a wide variety of ways, forms and materials. The subject matter of each body of work determines the material and form for the work. Found objects, paper, neon, wood, syringes, clothing tags, Swarovski crystals, ice, French fries, wine corks, condoms, and cigarettes are just some of the materials used to inspire, motivate, convey powerful statements and start a conversation.

The handcrafted process goes beyond the pen and paper adventure into the world of imagination, new processes and techniques. This is a precarious balancing act. In the process, designers may lose control over the end product, often leading them to interesting results thanks to happy accidents. The final pieces are left with their fingerprints and a sense of honesty translated by the handcrafted process into the reader's head. This makes handcrafted typography unconventional, playful, fluent, inviting and exciting.

The interaction of the piece and the audience is the moment typography comes to life because the beauty and purpose of creating text is never to remain unread. It requires the reader's conscious participation. The selection of materials creates value in the piece and invites people to engage with it. It incites a private affair with the reader even if the room is full of people.

Audiences will never be reluctant to embrace the revolutionary changes of handcrafted typography due to its capability of evolving with its society, time and era. Type is shaped due to the intuitive craftsmanship of the young typographic warriors that believe that being like everyone else leads to mediocrity and being boring and irrelevant rather than evoking newness, surprise, and excitement.

Handcrafted artistic typography invites thought as well as direct communication that creates and preserves social links. The artistic process and story behind a piece is what engages, intrigues and captures the imagination of viewers leading to a mutual respect between the work and the audience. Handcrafting typefaces is an intimate process of turning letters into images with spirit, that will continue to transform our society, the way we look at things and how we interact with art, only if as young typographic warriors we are willing to keep pushing our boundaries.

The Value and Importance of Handcrafted Type

Dave Greasley, Creative Partner @ Side by Side, UK

Handcrafted type has become the next inevitable step for designers striving to push boundaries. Simply taking type from a 2D environment, like paper or screen, into the real world unlocks an infinite number of outcomes. With designers struggling to stand out in a digital age, stepping away from the computer has proven to be the answer.

The mixture of typography with substance can bring a flat piece of design to life. It allows the audience to interact with a piece and can evoke reactions that cannot be brought on by type alone. The word honey, dripping in glistening, runny, golden honey will always be more appealing than the word simply typeset in a nice font.

Handcrafted work often has subtle imperfections, which only add to the authenticity of the design. It is these faults that show the viewer the piece is real and that many hours have gone into constructing it. It is important to not over-edit these typographic pieces, for fear they will appear more like 3D renders.

The scale of this handcrafted type revolution spans from the microscopic NYC Subway typography by Craig Ward to the world's largest poster, made for Malmo Festival by Stockholm-based SNASK. We also have influential figures such as Stefan Sagmeister whose studio took a year away from client work to create "Things I Have Learned" — a book covering all manner of handmade typographic responses to this question.

With thousands of great typefaces available online, it can often seem too easy to simply pick one for your design. This has led to designers looking back to freehand forms of lettering such as signwriting to inspire their handcrafted pieces. As with any other new craft there's a big learning curve involved. Many pieces require reworking, due to the unknown nature of their matter. This means that time is a very important requirement. Allow time for mistakes and time to fully test and understand your substance when quoting a new job.

To stay ahead of the game today's graphic designer needs to be as comfortable with a drill, chisel, or tweezers, as they are with a pencil or mouse.

What's next in Handcrafted Type?

There's been a huge rise in food typography over the last couple of years. This stems from food being relatively cheap to work with, readily available and usually very pliable. Artists like Marmalade Bleue and Becca Clason have carved out a niche in this area and are reaping the rewards of being the "go-to" food typographers. They are furthering their skill set by creating stop-motion and time-lapse videos of their work in progress.

Creating these typographic pieces purely for social networking is also on the rise. The playful imagery is easy to consume, like and retweet, and has been used by UK supermarket chain Sainsbury's in their latest campaign with Side by Side: "Twist Your Favourites." The rise of social media, and in particular Instagram has only made handcrafted type more popular, with curated typography accounts pulling in followers of over half a million. People love looking at typography. Social media channels also enable people who may not necessarily have a design background to interact with and create type pieces, as the lines continue to be blurred between art and design.

This trend isn't likely to stop any time soon. It's a natural progression in design to explore new ways of being creative. Opening your mind to working with new materials is the next logical step in the constant pursuit of effective graphic communication. In many cases, the best pieces use materials in ways people have never seen before, which usually results in an "I wish I'd thought of that" moment.

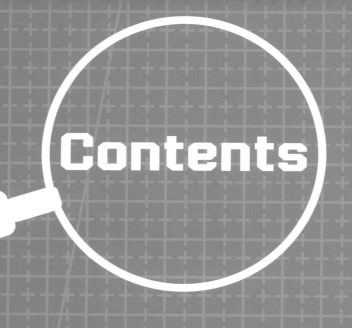

Contents

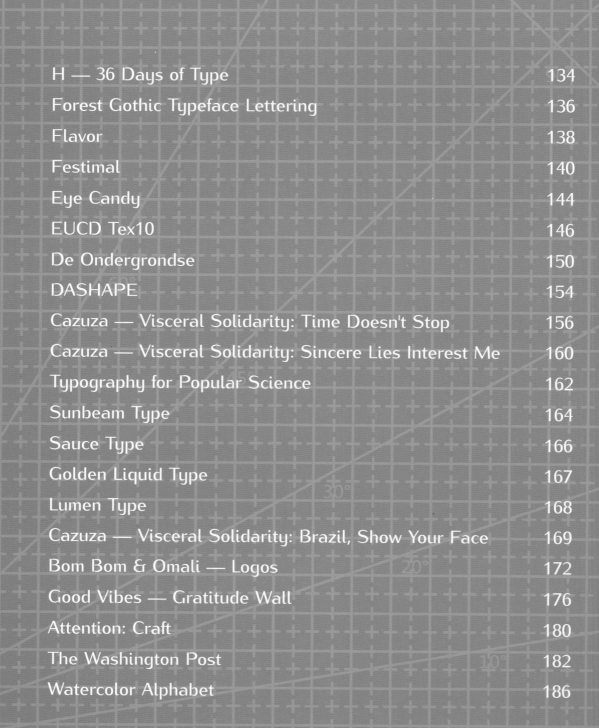

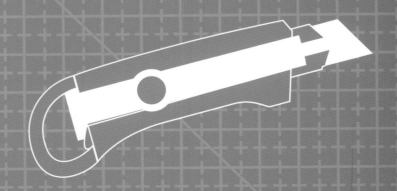

Wanto3 Aroma Living

Design Agency
Client   Silent Fragrance Industrial Co., Ltd.

"Wanto3" is based on aroma and pursues the harmony of relationship between "you, me and him/her." The composition of "sunlight, air and water" is balanced through the immersion of the most natural "body, mind and soul" extracted from the human body. The identification design is taken from the "W" and "3" with similar shapes to conduct design transformation, where the proper spacing and breath between words and lines manifests the natural air flow in daily life.

Materials & tools

paper, pencil, flower, scissors, camera, Photoshop

Process

1. Create the font style, depicting the possible look stroke by stroke.

2. Add flower and fruit as materials, using technical pen to depict the font image of "3."

3. Collect suitable flowery materials and think over the suitable layout style and combination.

4. Implement an organic artistic design, following the shape of "3" to place flowers on the proper positions.

5. Design completed. Repeatedly review and adjust the image angle to validate the shape.

6. Take photos of the text image in different tones through Spring/Summer and Autumn/Winter.

7. Conduct post-processing until the elegant font image design is completed.

8. Apply the image to different carriers to present a complete visual atmosphere.

7	1	2
	3	4
8	5	6

Tartufo — Food Art & Typography

Designer Anna Keville Joyce
Photographer Agustín Nieto

Client Tartufo

This project is a 3-part food art & typography series inspired by the foundations of geometric forms. Each image in the series played on an individual geometric shape — square, circle, and triangle. The series was created entirely out of food ingredients.

Materials & tools

cardboard stencil, food ingredients, food styling tools, paintbrush, spatulas, dental tools

Process

1. Create a lightweight cardboard stencil of the basic typographic form.

2. Fill the stencil with different spice powder selections and, once removed, clean up the borders of the typeface using paintbrushes and spatulas.

3. Gather different food ingredient elements to use in the composition.

4. Compose different design elements in and around the typeface using food ingredients, either freehand or using stencil patterns.

5. Tidy up and finish the design elements freehand using different painting, dental, and food styling tools.

1	2	3b	4
3a		5	

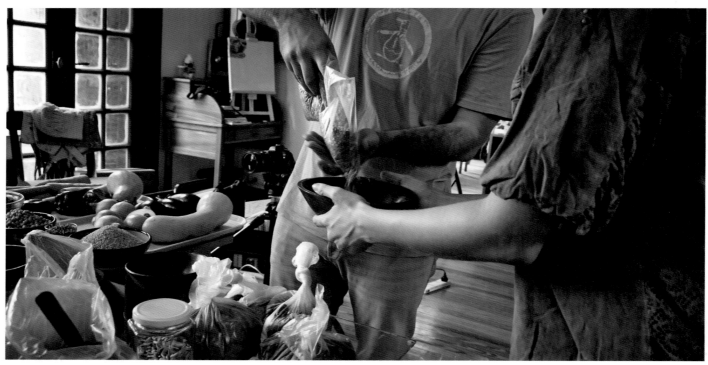

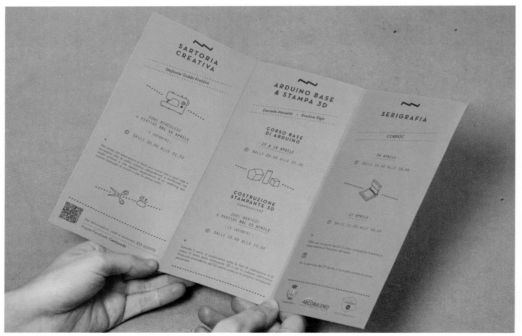

Workshop 2014, Cantiere 26 — Brochure

Art Director & Designer Francesca Pasini   *Client* Cantiere 26, Youth Center Arco (TN), Italy
Photographer Christian Parolari

This project is the brochure design promoting a 2014 workshop of Cantiere 26 youth center. The designer created this brochure using three different techniques connected to the three brochure topics: a workshop about fashion design, one about 3D printing and one about silk-screen printing.

Materials & tools

plasticine, needlework, solvent transfer from photocopy

Process

1. Select the right fonts, create the layout, and chose the colors and the techniques to create 3D handcrafted typography.

2. Creation of "WORKSHOP", as a result of solvent transfer from photocopy.

3. Creation of "APRILE 2014": a needlework typography. Draw the text on cardboard, pierce the paper to make sewing easier, and sew the cardboard following the drawn type.

4. Create the type "Cantiere 26": look at the photocopy reference and model the plasticine to make the letters.

5. Set creation: fix the cardboard on the table and position the plasticine's type below the first two types.

1	2	3c	
3a	3b	4	5

Quillography

Designer   Lori Lennon
Photographer   Bill Lennon

The object of this project was to recreate a font through a handmade technique. Starting from the concept of "quillography," the designer selected these simple materials and tools and created this amazing piece of artistic work.

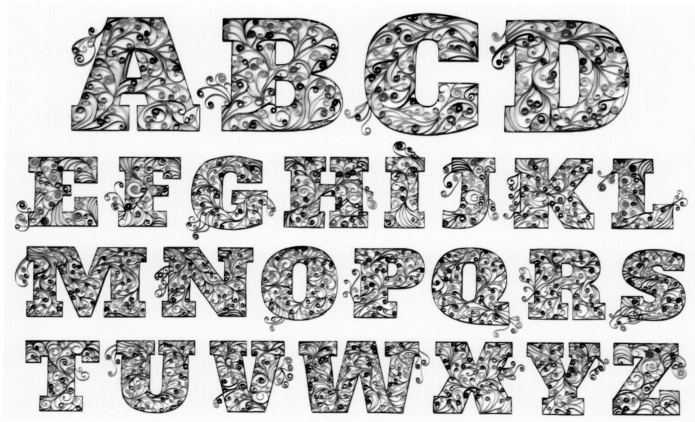

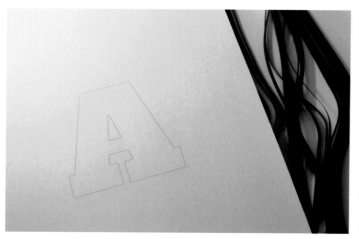

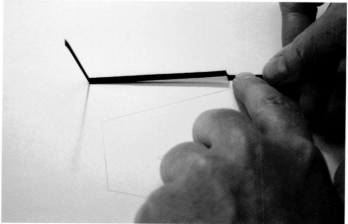

 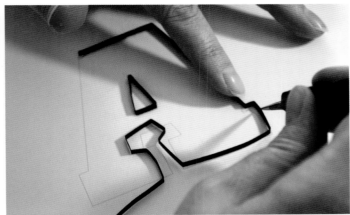

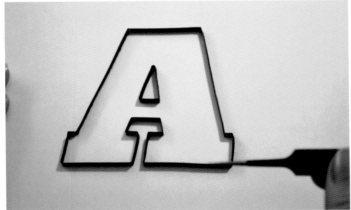 

		3	4
1	2	5	6
		7	

Materials & tools

quilling paper, quilling tool, piercing tool, tweezers, scissors, small ruler, glue, cardstock, computer, and printe

Process

1. Select your typeface and outline the letter with a very thin and lightly colored stroke. Center the letter on the page and print on cardstock.
2. Select the color, bend and fold the paper along the entire outline.
3. Apply a thin line of glue along the outline.
4. Using the tweezers, carefully apply your pre-shaped letter onto the glue line.
5. Work around the entire letter and then let dry completely .
6. Make curls and shapes to fill your letter with and apply a small amount of glue to the bottom edge.
7. Place the curls/shapes in the letterform.

Ludo Sans Typeface

Designer   David Luepschen, Janina Sitzmann

The project, an animated typeface, highlights the duo's shared passion for typography while exploring their joint interest in nontraditional animation. Ludo Sans by definition is a handcrafted sans serif typeface. The Strata-Cut method — a form of stop motion invented during the 1920s and 1930s by German animator Oskar Fischinger — was used to bring a level of arbitrary playfulness to the process while delivering an experimental composition unique to the approach. For video and more information: http://ow.ly/UyaR8.

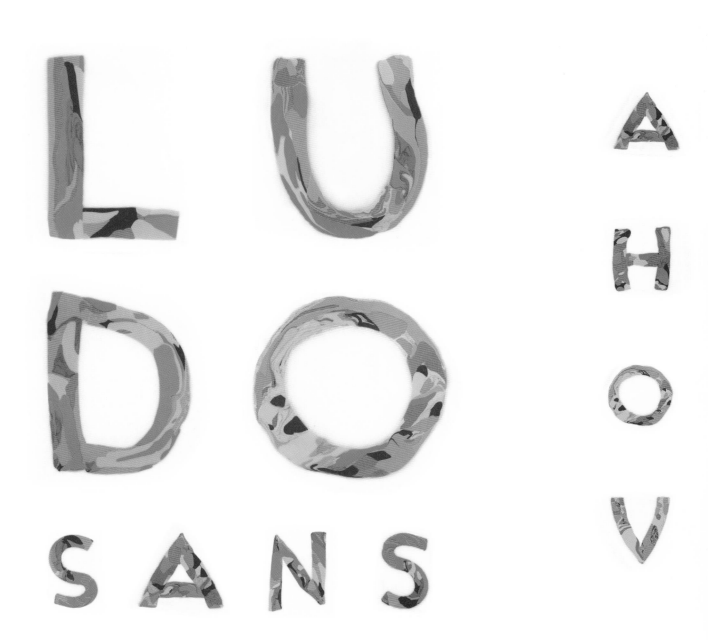

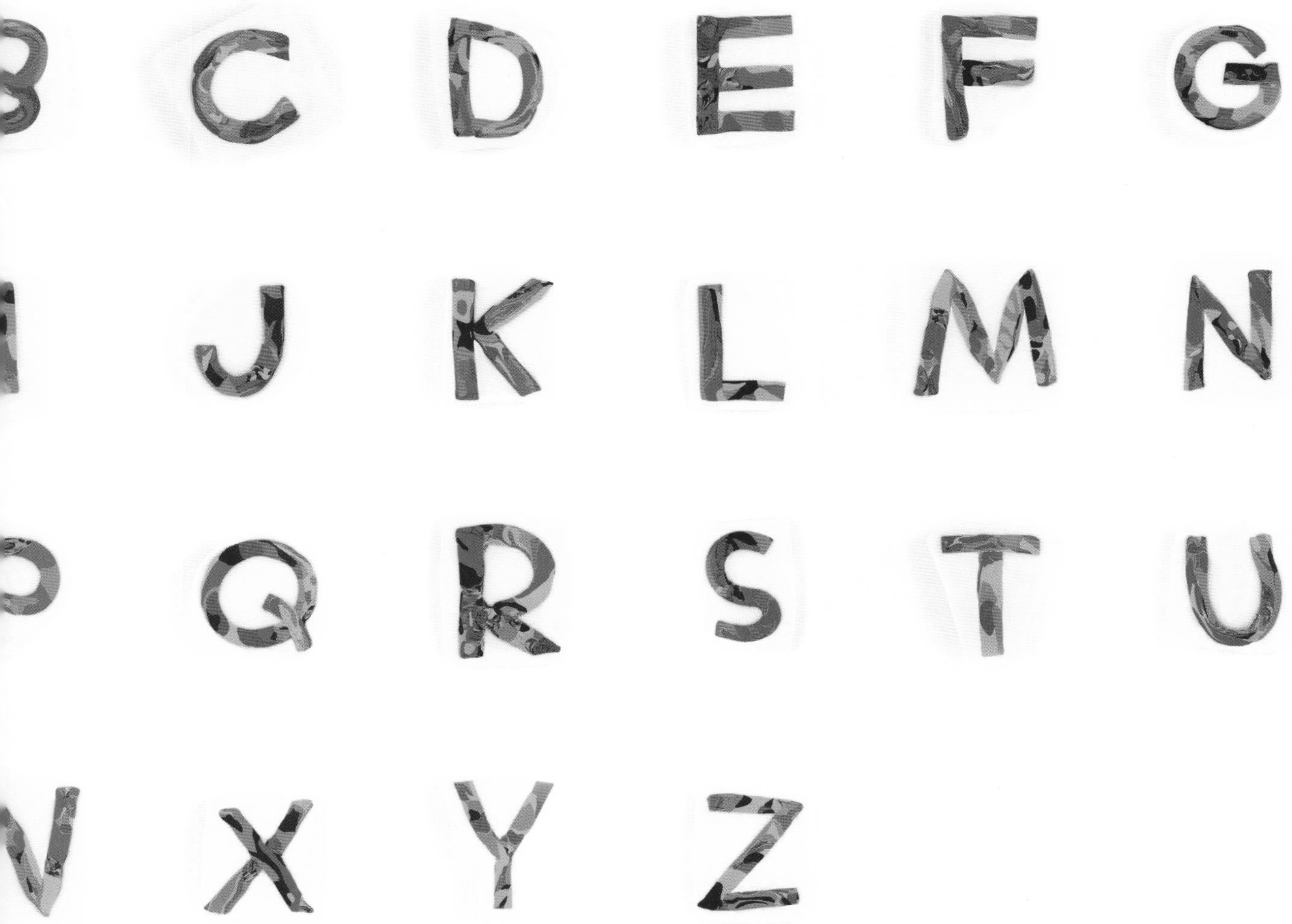

B C D E F G

H I J K L M N

P Q R S T U

V X Y Z

Materials & tools

Plasticine, wax, white pigments, knife, photo camera, light

Process

1. Model the Ludo Sans typeface out of multi-colored strands of plasticine.

2. Arrange the letters in lines and rows according to the alphabet.

3. Cast each letter in wax to a "loaf" and set aside to dry.

4. For the stop motion animation, slice each letter very thinly and take a picture of the "loaf" after each cut.

1a	1b	2b	2c
		3	4a
2a		4b	4c

Blossom Type

Designer   Nikita Schukin, Alice Mourou
Design Agency Zero Agency

This project is about the alphabet and is inspired by flower blossoms. All letters are handcrafted using natural flowers, and Photoshop has been used for retouch and color correction.

Materials & tools

natural flowers, floristry materials, floristry tools

Process

1. Sketch all letterforms on paper.
2. Get all the materials and tools ready.
3. Construct each letter out of natural flowers following the sketches.
4. Shoot photos of the letters and retouch them in Photoshop.

1a	1b	
2a	2b	4
3a	3b	

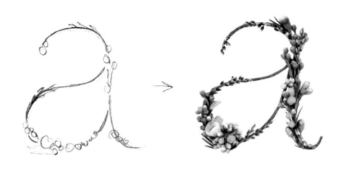

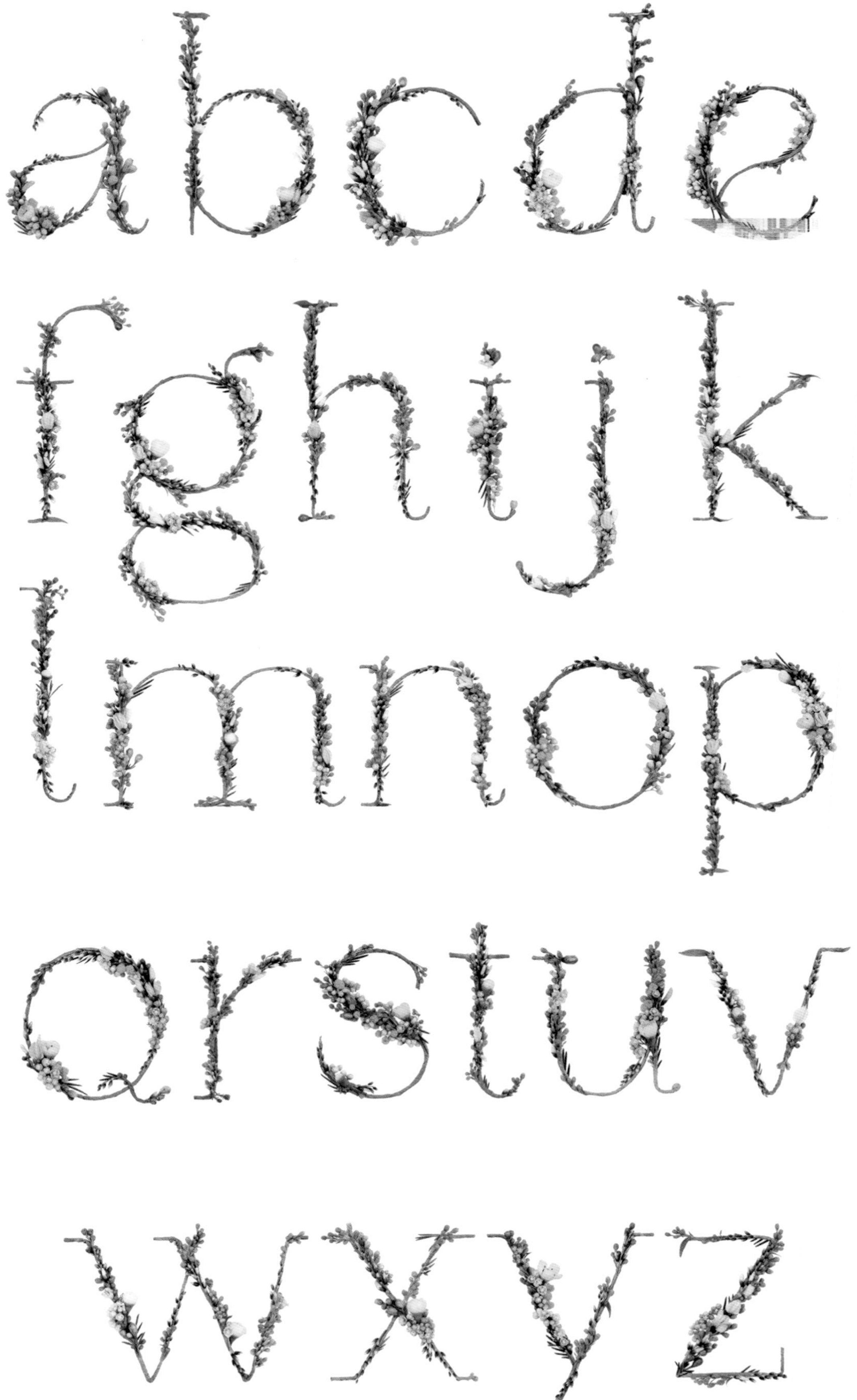

abcde
fghijk
lmnop
qrstuv
wxyz

Wire Type

Designer   Ana Gomez Bernaus

This project originated in the desire to create a material typeface by hand. The material's behavior and its characteristics helped shape the look and feel of the resulting piece.

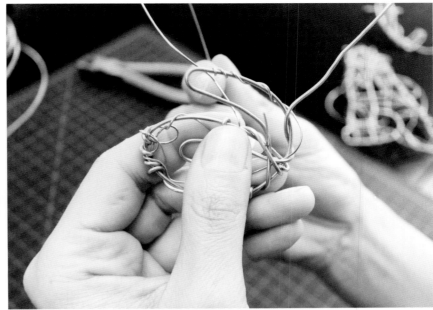
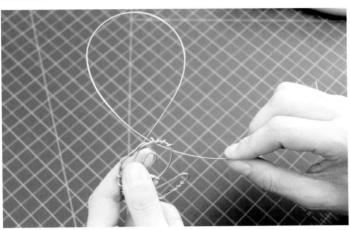
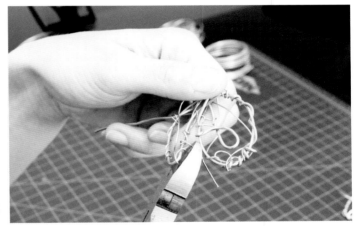

	1	2a
4	2b	3a
		3b

Materials & tools

copper wire, pliers

Process

1. Model the basic shape of each letter with a thicker wire.

2. Add details to the interior of the letter with a thinner wire.

3. Use the pliers to make sure that the thinner wire details are well composed in each letter.

4. Connect all letters to form the sentence.

#tipocalialfabeto

Designer   Thiago Reginato

The #tipocalialfabeto project is a multi-layer alphabet that was born from a mixture of techniques, textures, and references, mainly nature. It is an experimental project that was applied to posters and clothes.

Materials & tools

paper, ink, pen, source materials

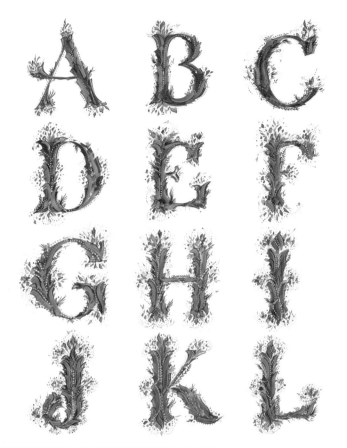

San Diego Latino Film Festival Poster

Designer   Rodrigo Zarain Rojas   *Client*   Media Arts Center San Diego
Design Agency   Rodzarain

This project is a poster created for the contest at the Media Arts Center of San Diego, California 2015. The main idea was to make a poster by hand. The designer put on some good tunes and started making letters out of clay. He decided to make different types of fonts, taking inspiration from music festivals, albums, etc.

Materials & tools

white clay, wooden desk, camera, Photoshop, Illustrator

Process

1. Use the white clay to model the icons related to the festival and the title fonts.

2. Arrange the icons and fonts on the wooden desk to get the layout.

3. Take photos and import them into Photoshop, and paint using a Wacom tablet for the perfect colors. Import to Illustrator to add the word festival and the information.

1		
2a	2b	3
2c	2d	

Morris — Wooden Letterpress Typeface

Designer Therese Ølberg

In this project, the designer created a new typeface inspired by William Morris' dedication to and love for nature. The different illustrations inside each letter are inspired by his wallpaper designs. The typeface is based on the font "Bodoni Old Face bold." All the letters are designed in Illustrator, then cut out in wood using a laser cutter, and finally the wooden letters are placed on a letterpress to print the letters onto paper. By using this technique you can make beautiful letters to create unique and creative letters.

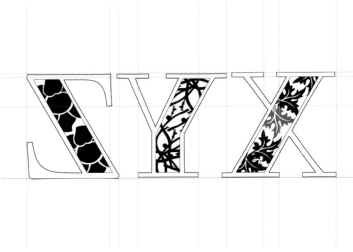

Materials & tools

wood square, sandpaper, ink, paper, letterpress, glue, varnish, laser cutter

Process

1. Find inspiration, draw illustrations and make a pattern.

2. Select your typeface, use pieces of the pattern to place inside the letters. Make the typeface ready for the laser cutter and remember to reflect all the letters vertically. That way the letters will be printed the right way on the final print.

3. Cut and engrave the letters using a laser cutter.

4. Sand the outside edges and the face of the letters to get a smooth surface. Put some wood glue on the backside of the letters and attach each letter to a wooden square. The square should be about the same size as the letter.

5. Use a brush to cover the letters with varnish to protect the wood square.

6. Arrange the letters on a board, as you want them to appear on the final print.

7. Roll a thin layer of ink onto each letter, place a piece of paper on top of the letters and use the letterpress to print.

1	2	4	
		5	7
3		6	

Encantos de Cordel

Designer   Juliana Zarattini, Artur Mello Lattaro   *Client*   Luiz Pedro Simoni (Canarinhos Da Terra)
Design Agency   Melt Design

The Encantos de Cordel musical (Canarinhos da Terra Project — Unicamp) needed the creation of a visual identity to promote their performances in Brazil. The designers were inspired by the "cordel" (a type of Brazilian literature, literally "string hung literature"), and its visual elements. For the brand, they recreated handmade letters, as if they had been carved into wood. The rest of the alphabet was designed in order to harmonize with the other parts.

ABCDEFGHIJKL
MNOPQRSTuvxZ

DIREÇÃO E CRIAÇÃO

DIREÇÃO MUSICAL: VASTI ATIQUE
DIREÇÃO EXECUTIVA: LUIZ PEDRO SIMONI / ERIK EKSTROM
DIREÇÃO CÊNICA: MARCELO PERONI / CAROL FERRETI
FIGURINOS: MARIA ELENA H. SIMONI
CENOGRAFIA: JULIANA FERNANDES
TEXTO: ROSANGELA PERONI BRIGONI

EQUIPE MUSICAL

REGÊNCIA: VASTI ATIQUE / RAFAEL K. KASHIMA
REGÊNCIA, PIANO E FLAUTA: CLEO BRANCO
REGÊNCIA, PIANO: SANDRA MARA VICENTE
PIANO: THAIS TEIXEIRA FABBRI
MUSICALIZAÇÃO E TEORIA MUSICAL: RITA TADDEI
PREPARAÇÃO VOCAL: ELISABETE ALMEIDA
OFICINAS DE PERCUSSÃO E PERCUSSIONISTA: DANTAS NEVES RAMPIN
SANFONEIRO: JUAREZ PEREIRA CARVALHO - "JUAREZ DE CARNAÍBA"

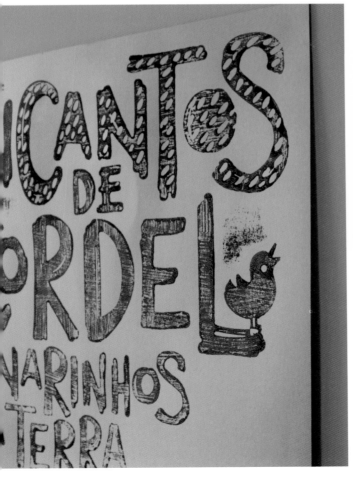

1		4a	
2	3a		
3b		4b	4c

Materials & tools

paper, wood, ink, brush

Process

1. Draw the letters and scan to turn them into vector.
2. Create the piece of wood.
3. Paint the embossed parts with ink.
4. Press against the paper to print the letters.

Mit Franz und Gloria — Lasercut Letterpress

Art Director   Andreas Hogan
Designer   Caroline Birkel

This is an experimental typography and printing project. Inspired by old posters and advertisements, the designer created two new and very different fonts. "Franz" is a script font created from her handwriting with a thin brush while "Gloria" is a sans serif font in different weights and is especially appropriate for posters and printing in large formats.

ALTER
KNABE
KNABE
ALTER

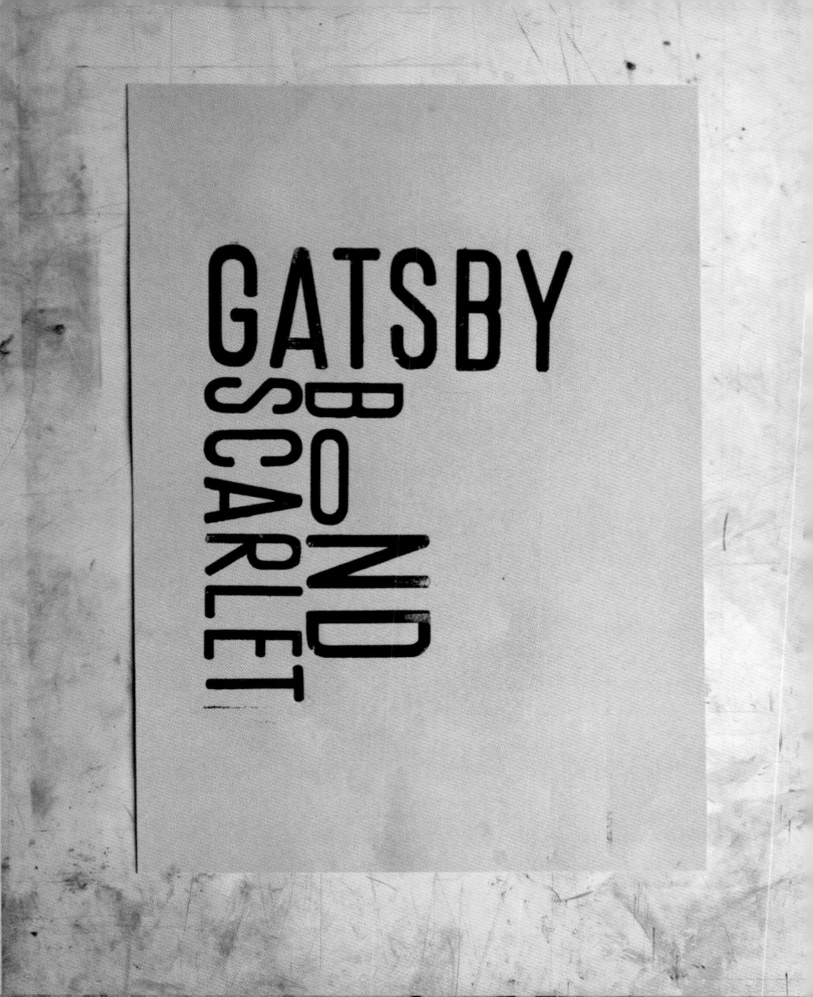

GATSBY
BOND
SCARLET

DRAMA
LOSS
HATE
LOVE

SPIELS
NOCH
EINMAL
SAM

45

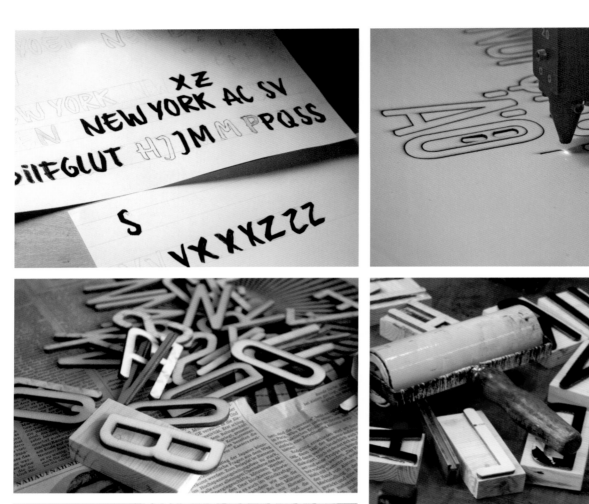

Materials & tools

thin brush, thin panel, laser cutter, hand-lever press

1	2a	4b
2b	3a	
3		5

Process

1. Create your font. Scan in your sketches and transform them into paths.

2. Use a laser cutter to cut all letters into thin panels of wood.
   The wood should be at least 5mm thick, so it won't break while printing.

3. Glue the letters onto precisely measured blocks of hardwood and let them dry;
   put some pressure to make sure they will hold. Don't forget to mirror them
   when you are gluing them on.

4. Put the letters together in the sentence and fix with magnets and metal parts
   onto the hand-lever press. Roll the printing ink onto them and clean dirty edges
   before printing. Carefully lay the paper on the woodletters and start printing.

5. Slowly strip off the paper from the woodletters.

Wild Potato

Designer   Ivan Alves
Design Agency   Nor267

As creatives who love challenges, for this project the designers at Nor267 got off the computer screens and approached it in a different way, creating a typeface made from handcrafted potato stamps.

After three days of cutting, drying, painting, stamping and drying, the alphabet was finally completed. Then all the letters were scanned and turned into a digital font, which was named "Wild Potato."

HI THERE
LOREM IPSUM
AÇORDA
HAMBURGER
& POTATOES
SPECIMEN
OLÁ EU SOU UMA BATATA
NOR 267

QUICK BROWN POTAT
NOT MY TYPI
1984
CERVEJA ARTESANA
HANDMADE
JOSÉ SARAMAGO
PORTO
21ST CENTURY

ABCDEFGHIJKLMNOPQRSTUVWXYZ
ABCDEFGHIJKLMNOPQRSTUVWXYZ
ÀÁÂÃÇÉÊÍÓÔÕÚ
ÀÁÂÃÇÉÊÍÓÔÕÚ
Ø123456789
&©®×»«˜ˆ˜ˊ\/€!#+%@.:=
$}{)(_–---•,;<><>*?""""|||||

Materials & tools

potatoes, cutting tools, ink, paper, scanner

Process

1. Cut the potatoes in half and drain their juice.

2. Sculpt a mirrored version of every letter on each potato.

3. Paint the sculpted letter surface with acrylic paint and let it dry out.

4. Take a few close-up photos of the drying potatoes.

5. Start stamping away each letter a couple of times on paper.

6. Make a few posters before trashing the potatoes.

7. Scan the stamped letters to create the digital font.

8. Convert the scanned letters into vectors to create the complete digital font.

7	1	2
	3	4
8	5	6

Wired Magazine UK Masthead

Designer	Gerard Miró
Design Agency	Lo Siento

Client   Wired Magazine UK/Condé Nast

This project is the masthead design for Wired magazine UK. To create the Wired logo in a different way, Lo Siento handcrafted all the letters: sketching, cutting, assembling, photographing and retouching.

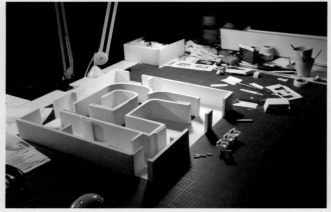

	5		
1	2		4
3a	3b		

Materials & tools

cardboard, cutter, fast glue, camera

Process

1. Sketch the Wired logo, and mark out the dimensions on the cardboard.
2. Cut all the elements out of the cardboard by hand, with each letter approximately 50x50 cm.
3. Assemble all the elements and use a fast glue to accelerate the process.
4. Complete the structure.
5. All characters are photographed separately and then turned into vectors for retouching.

Type Experiment (Thread 1)

Designer Filipe Lizardo

The designer used the phrase "Nowhere to go" as a statement of mind for beginning an introspective design process, revealing the experience itself locked into a grid. Step-by-step he discovered unlimited opportunities to construct new meanings. Type and life seem mixed in the same path. Creativity can always shift what seems unchangeable!

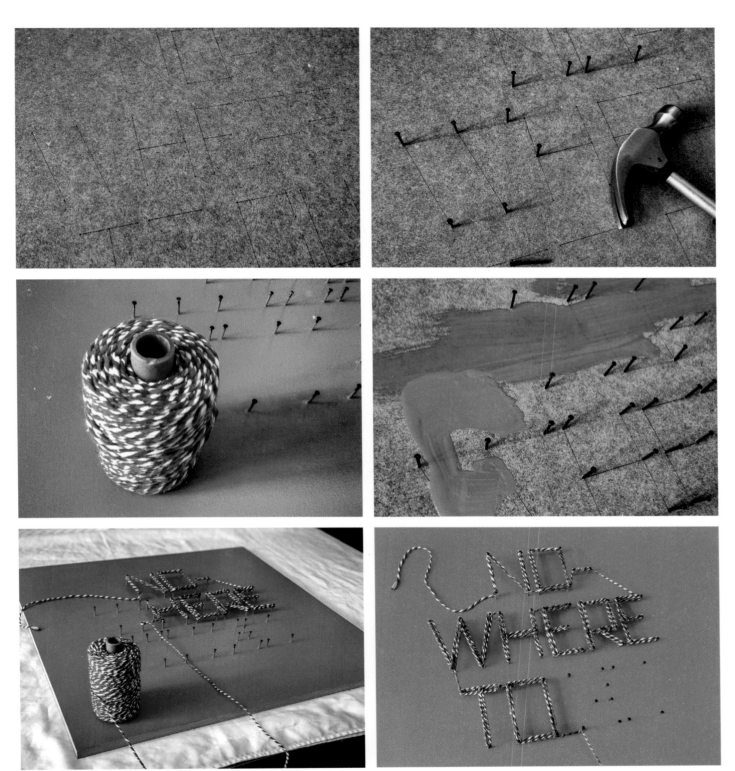

Materials & tools

wooden board, nails, tri-colored baker's twine, acrylic paint

Process

1. Draw a geometric uppercase display typeface with a thin line width, highlight the key points of each letter, and transfer it onto a wooden board using carbon paper.

2. With the typeface traced, nail all the key points.

3. Paint the board with the main color red based on the tri-colored baker's twine.

4. Connect the nails with the baker's twine. Make a sequence and sometimes repeat the path, character-by-character, to give shape to and reveal the type structure.

5. Words become visible and linked with a three-dimensional use of space.

	1	2
5	3a	3b
	4a	4b

Remember We are Trash

Designer   Giulio Mosca

Remember We are Trash is the first of a poster series called "Remember
What We are", a huge work the designer completed; more will be released
soon. The typography is made of real trash taken from a real dustbin,
taking 12 hours. The smell was horrible! But it's okay, because we are also
this: TRASH.

Materials & tools

trash, paper, Illustrator, camera

Process

1. Find the materials you want to use to create your "real stuff poster"
   (in this case real trash from a real dustbin).

2. Design the poster in Adobe Illustrator. Print the letters or words on paper and place them on the floor
   (or background you want to use). Do not fill the letters; use a stroke as your guideline.

3. Build the letters with the trash following the printed outline font.

4. Photograph the words and poster.

5. Post-process your images to create the entire poster.

	1	2
5	3	4

Pennies Typeface

Designer   Muneebah Waheed

With the purpose of creating a bespoke typeface for an exhibition celebrating type design at the Design Museum, the designer chose coins which are easily accessible and handmade a set of letters and a series of posters.

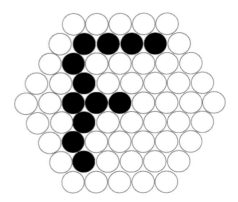

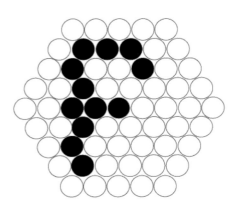

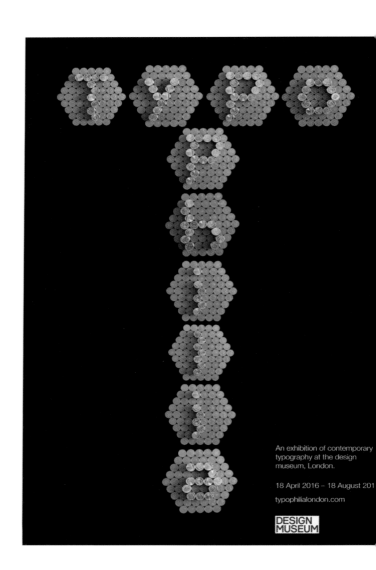

An exhibition of contemporary typography at the design museum, London.

18 April 2016 – 18 August 201

typophilialondon.com

DESIGN MUSEUM

Materials & tools

British penny, camera, Photoshop

Process

1. Create a grid using circles, plan where your coins will go to create the letterforms, and print this out.

2. Separate your coins in shiny and dull. Assemble your dull coins in this grid format on your surface. Then create piles of 10 shiny coins, tacking them in between so they won't slip when you inevitably knock them.

3. Follow your grid, assemble each letter at a time and photograph it in the same lighting.

4. Retouch the images with Photoshop for use on the final posters.

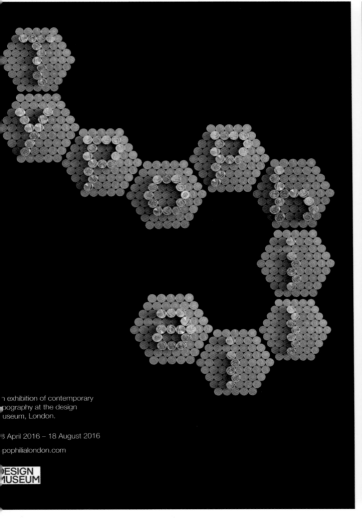

An exhibition of contemporary
typography at the design
museum, London.

8 April 2016 – 18 August 2016

opophilialondon.com

An exhibition of contemporary
typography at the design
museum, London.

18 April 2016 – 18 August 2016

typophilialondon.com

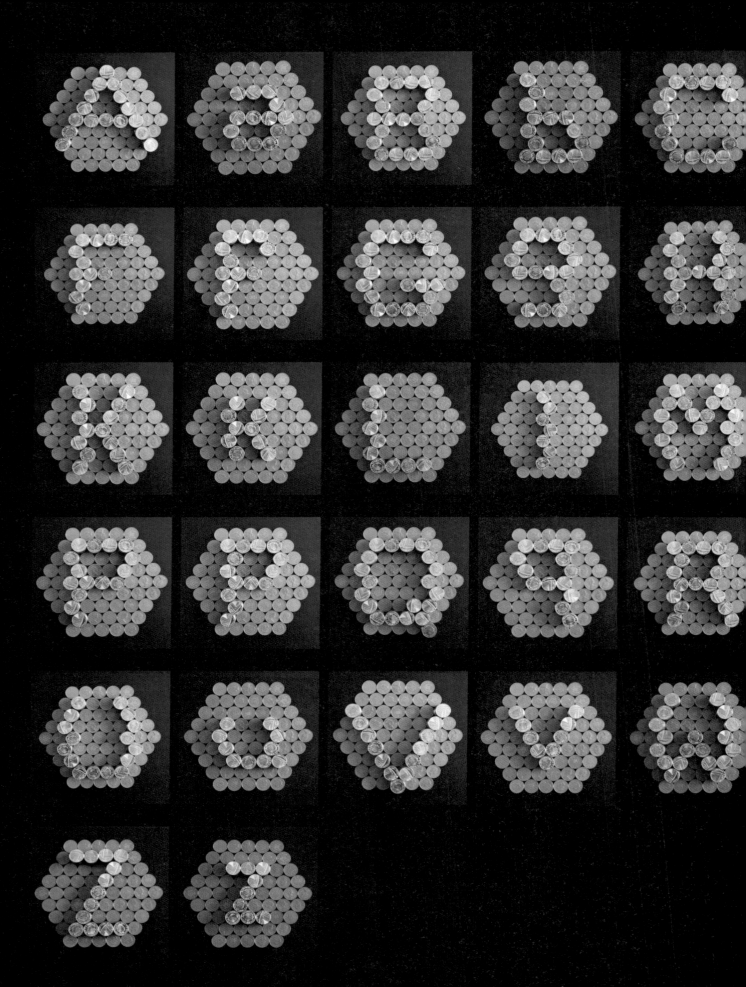

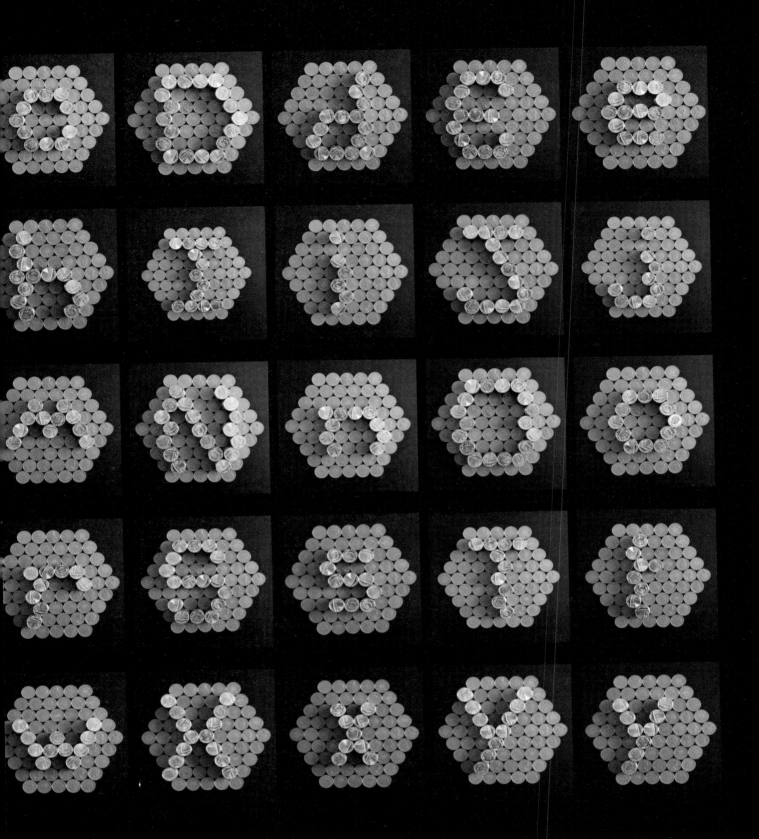

LOVE

Designer   Ceres Lau

In life, we focus too much on bigger things and forget how even the smallest gestures can make a meaningful impact. Thus this piece of art focuses on the little details, bringing out the significance behind the quote. What we do may be small in the grand scheme of things, but if it is done with love, really, that is what matters.

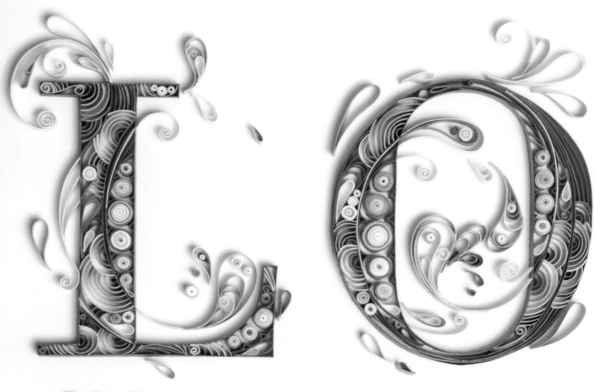

DO SMALL THINGS WITH GREAT

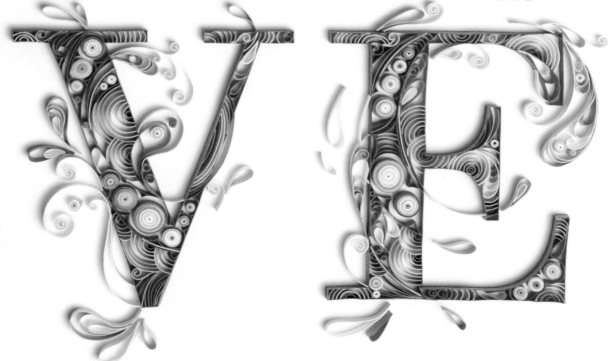

1	2
3	4

Materials & tools

quilling paper, quilling tools, scissors, tweezers, glue, plastic lid, toothpick, damp cloth

Process

1. Sketch and draw out all the details on the paper.

2. Trace the sketch lightly onto your artwork base and begin outlining the letters with strips of papers.

3. Fill in the red dividers inside the letters. Curl the strips slightly for easier manipulation and bending.

4. Start filling in the letters according to the design with colourful paper strips.

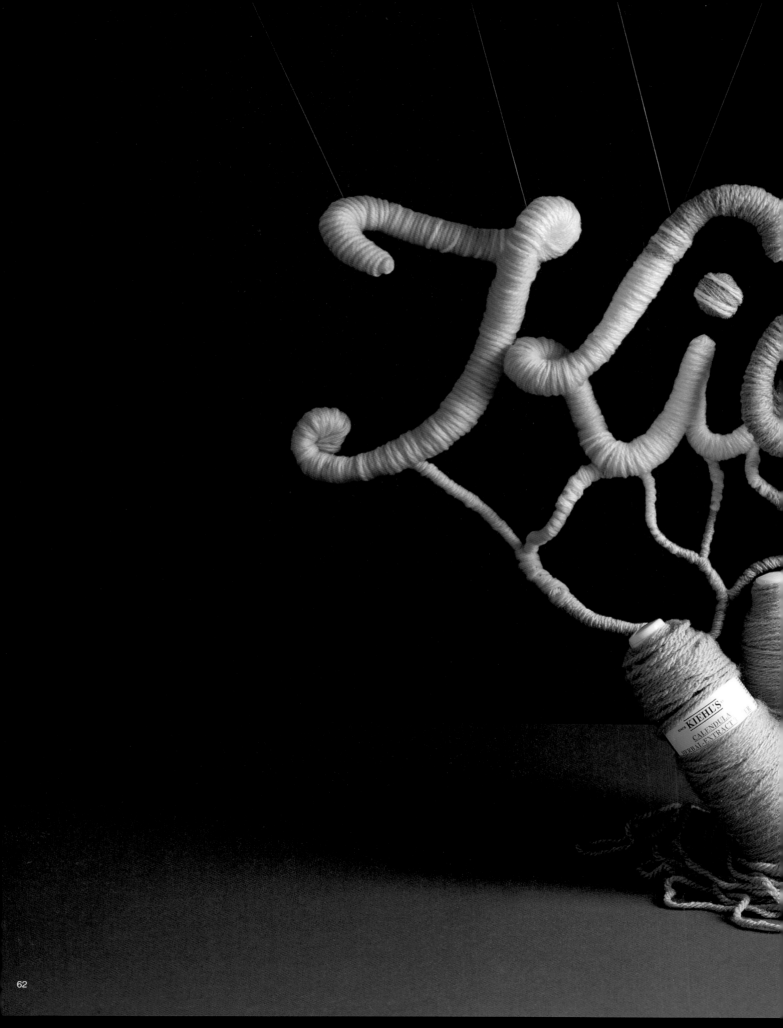

Kiehl's USA — Part of the Artfully Made Campaign

Designer   Noelia Lozano
Client   Kiehl's USA

This project is a handmade wool type still life visual composition commissioned by Kiehl's USA, part of the Artfully Made Campaign. It conveys the nature-oriented brand's focus on botany and cosmetics.

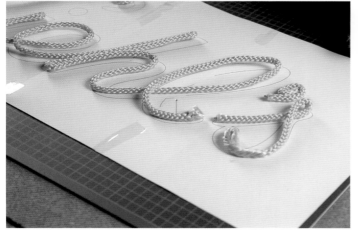

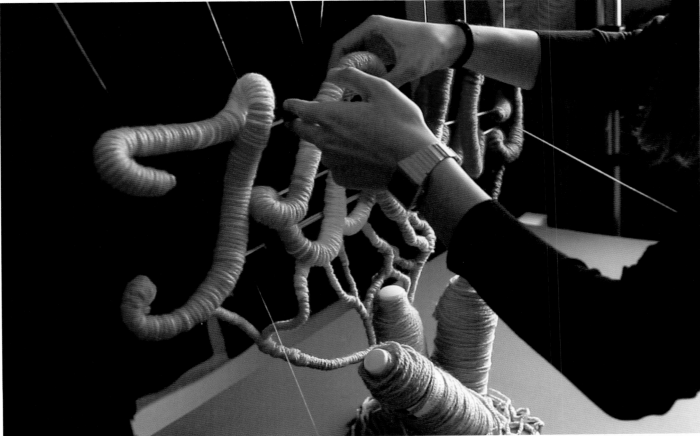

Materials & tools

colored wool, cord, wire, wooden sticks, needle, yarn, glue, pins, tape

Process

1. Get the materials ready; print the vectorized brand logo and use as a base for the lettering.

2. The wire will be the skeleton for the composition. Model the wire by hand, following the lettering.

3. Introduce the cord along the wire lettering, using it as the interior of the composition.

4. Thread the wool yarn around the lettering, and use pins and tape to adjust the wool.

5. Once the wool is rolled, adjust all the lettering by moving the wire.
   Use the wooden sticks to cross the lettering and give some consistency to the composition.

6. Compose your set for the final photo shoot.

7. Adjust the different parts of the composition. Retouch and adjust in Photoshop.

1a	1b	5	6
2			
3	4	7	

Kedeng Kedeng

Design Agency   Mals
Client   KOP, Graphic Design Festival Breda

The project is a typographic piece commissioned by KOP for a show called Oneliners. Studio Mals made an object out of wood, about 2×5 meters in size, using the words Kedeng Kedeng from a nationally famous song by local singer Guus Meeuwis. The words replicate the noise from a building next to the spot as well as train noise. It is also a cheeky homage to the much beloved Dutch singer.

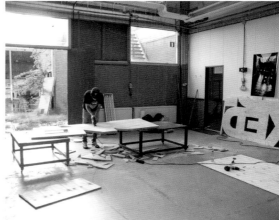

1	2	4a
3		4b

Materials & tools

wood, paint, powertools, hammer, nails

Process

1. Get the materials ready to use.

2. Draw the outline of the words "Kedeng Kedeng" on a piece of wood.
   Use the powertools to drill and cut the wood to form each part of the words.

3. Use a hammer and nails to join the wood to form the dimensional words.

4. Paint the words, let them dry, and install.

Garden, Flowers and Ice

Designer Manuel Persa

Inspired by colorful flowers during a nature walk, this typography project was developed by Manuel Persa. Through silicone molds, a fresh and minimalist image is created using ice and wild flowers.

4a	1a	
	1b	2
4b	3a	3b

Materials & tools

wild flowers, ice, silicone molds, water, freezer

Process

1. Wild and colorful flowers are taken from nature.

2. Wild flowers are selected and grouped together according to color.

3. The flowers are put into the silicone molds, and water is added. Finally the molds are put into the freezer.

4. Some time later, each letter is removed from its mold.

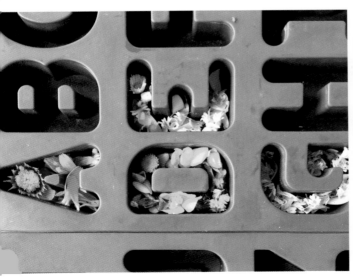

The Evolution of Type

Designer   Andreas Scheiger

Austrian designer Andreas Scheiger celebrates the "craft of etching, engraving and letter design" with a nod to both science and the graphic design of the Victorian era. Scheiger believes that letters are "full of life" and, in an effort to explore the means of communication by dissecting and rearranging its basic elements, he delves into the heart of typography with his sculptural letter series, The Evolution of Type.

Scheiger takes an anthropological look at the future of the craft. By carving into letters made of wood and crafting with polymer clay and bones, and castingletters and bones into plaster the designer spells out a cautionary tale that echoes the way of extinct species. With digital print processing, letterpress letters indeed become something like ancient species.

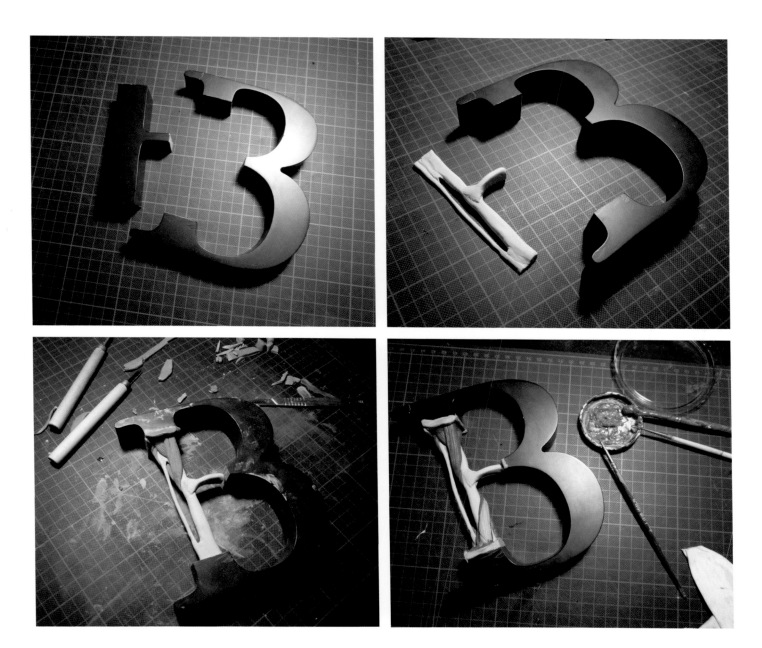

	1	2
	3	4

Materials & tools

wood, chicken bones, polymer clay, plaster, paint

Process

1. A letter is cut from wood and then cut into parts.

2. A chicken bone or similar is inserted as a replacement.

3. Muscles and tendons made of polymer clay are applied.

4. Paint is applied.

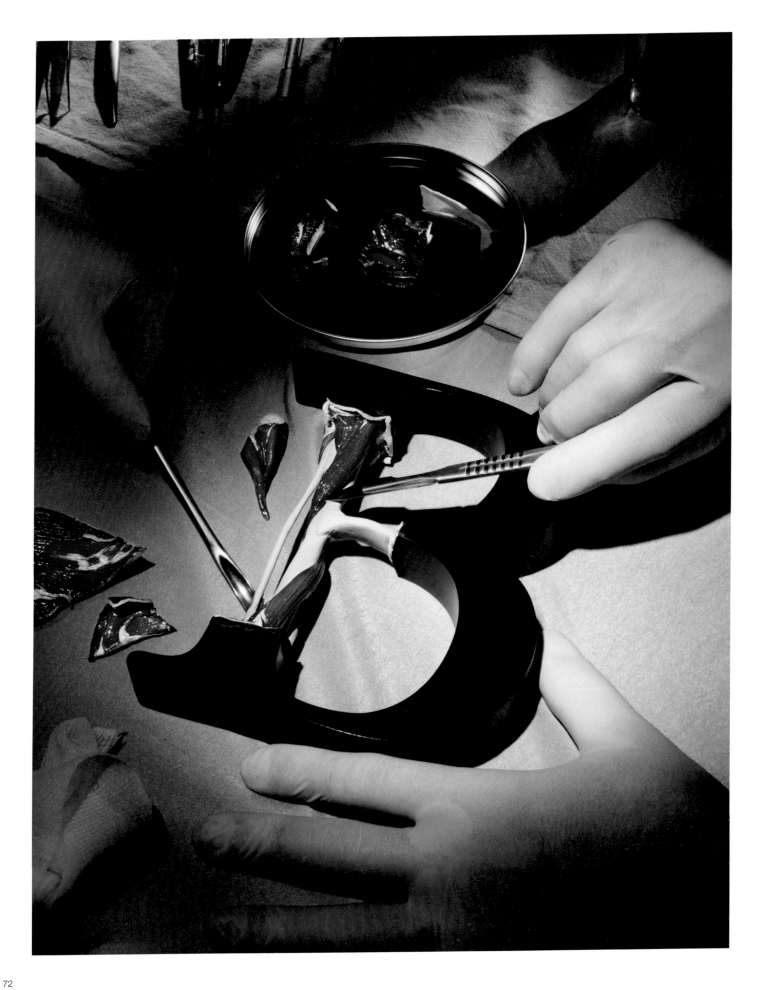

Process

1. A letter is cut out from a flat piece of wood.

2. Use this letter as a template, cut along the edge of the clay until a flat clay letter is obtained.

3. The letter is placed mirror-inverted onto a larger flat piece of clay. This will become the mold.

4. Various chicken bones are pressed into the letter and then removed, forming a skeleton pattern.

5. The mold's rim is applied. The mold is filled with liquid plaster.

6. The mold and the finished plaster fossilize.

7. Paint is applied.

8. The finished letter is photographed and digitalized.

8	1	2
	3	4
	5	6
		7

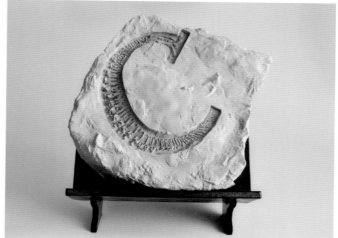

Evil Dead

Designer   Caylan Goring

This project was created with handmade elements. The concept to use concrete lettering was inspired by the film "Evil Dead" itself, to create something that showed the grit and personality of a horror film. The textures and tones from the concrete along with the shadows cast by the lighting bring the entire project together.

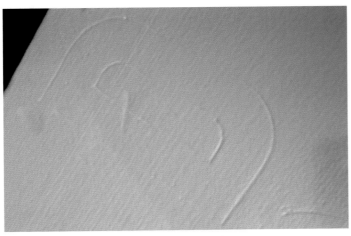

1	2
3	4
5	6

Materials & tools

concrete, polystyrene foam, duct tape, knife

Process

1. Create outline indentation of letter in the foam.

2. Cut out all the letters to create a stencil.

3. Place wood to act as base plate and secure down with duct tape.

4. Create a slurry mix with the concrete and fill in all the letters.

5. Carefully wipe away any excess concrete on the foam.

6. Once set, use a knife to gently cut away the foam from the letters.
   Finished letters are then photographed.

Don't Wait Create

Designer   Kelsey Layne

This project arose from the designer's personal design philosophy, 'Don't wait create' and was born through a combined love of handcrafted design and typography. To begin the process, the letterforms were sketched to scale along with the pattern designs. This ensured that the designs would be easily transferable when creating the final outcome.

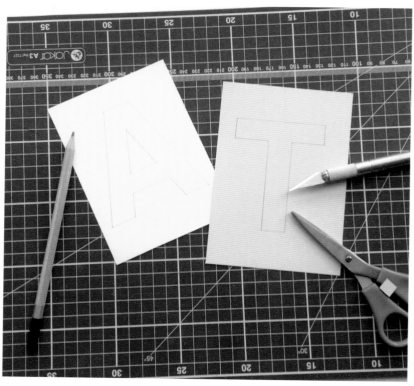

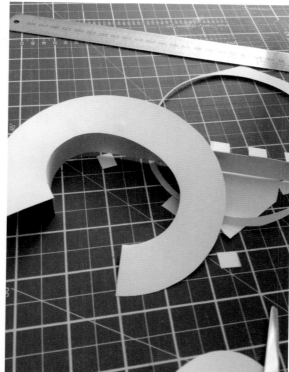

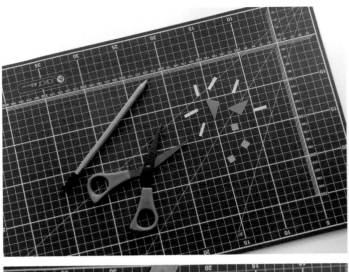

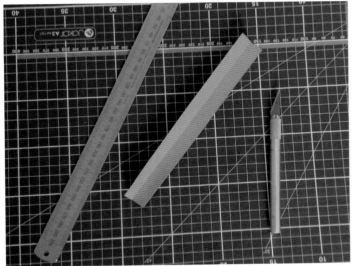

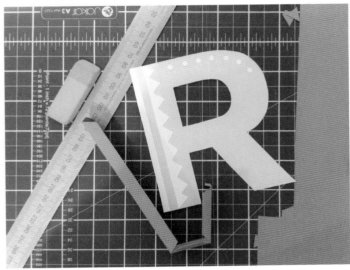

		2a	2b
		3	4
1a	1b	5	

Materials & tools

paper, card, scalpel, scissors, cutting mat, ruler, PVA glue

Process

1. Using a pencil, sketch the letterforms onto separate sheets of colored card and cut out using scissors or a scalpel.

2. Draw the shapes onto colored sheets of paper, and cut out and stick them onto the cut out letterforms with PVA glue.

3. Cut a strip out of colored card and fold it in half vertically.

4. Attach the face of the folded strip to the letterform without glue at this stage and bend the strip.

5. Attach the strip with PVA glue and repeat this process for each letterform.

Do Not Play with Your Food — Sweets and Candy

Designer   Alex Palazzi, Dani Raya

The idea was to unify design and sculpture. As a graphic designer and sculptor, Alex was looking for some experimentation with complex materials (candy in this case). Mixing typography and sculpture as the base of an exploration, the designers found that there are endless possibilities because nothing represents a product better than the product itself.

Materials & tools

clay, ice-cream, bubblegum, candy cotton, sculpting tools, camera, digital programs

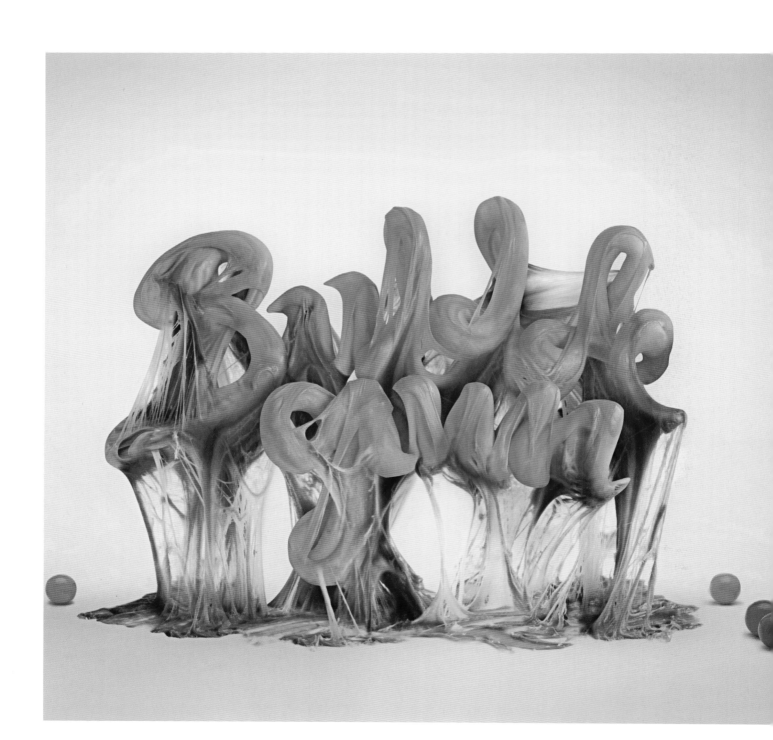

Process

1. Make a draft of the clay letter from a flat cut plastic reference.

2. Build up all letters.

3. Build up the letter holder.

4. Redefine the final letter look.

5. Put chewing gum on the letters for sticky simulation.

6. Make gum stick to the floor.

7. Finalize the art after photographing and retouching.

	1	2
7	3	4
	5	6

Process

1. Create a flat paper reference.
2. Carve all letters.
3. Insert the letters in their holders.
4. Redefine the letters.
5. Finalize the look of the letters.
6. Make the cotton candy.
7. Scoop up some cotton candy.
8. Put cotton candy on the lettering surface.
9. Drop sugar on the floor.
10. Finalize the art after photographing and retouching.

	10	3	4
		5	6
			7
1	2	8	9

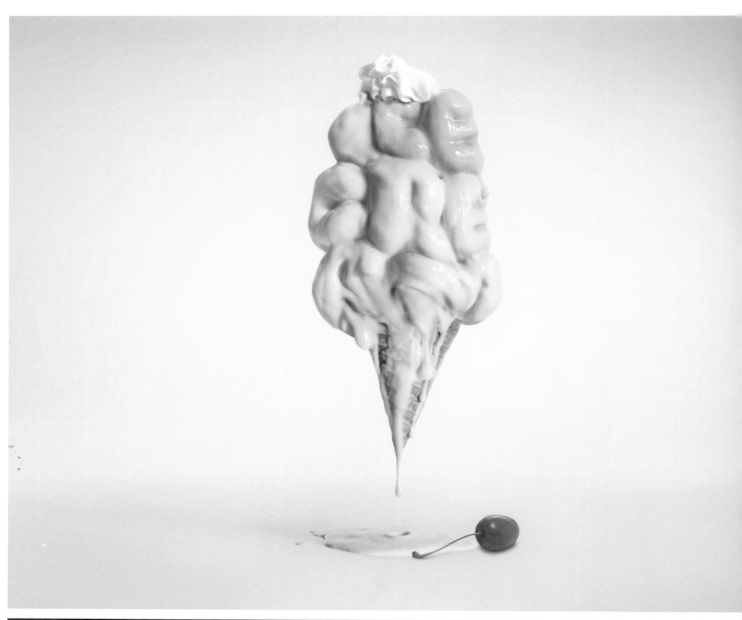

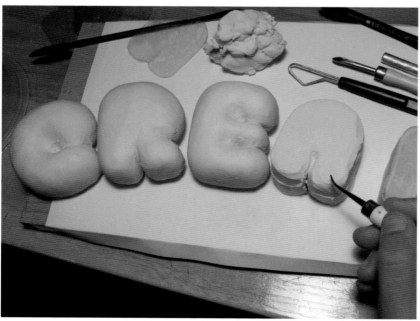

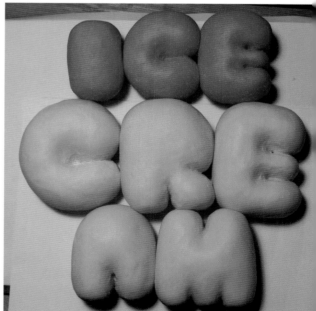

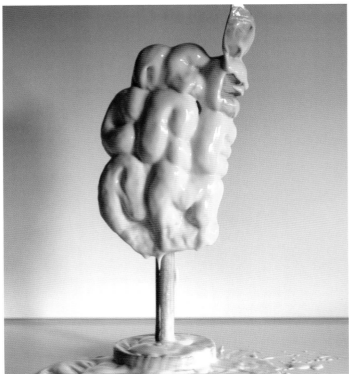

			3	4
8			5	6
1	2		7	

Process

1. Make clay letters from a flat cut plastic reference.
2. Finish letters.
3. Put the letters on a holder.
4. Drop vanilla ice-cream on the bottom part of the lettering.
5. Drop strawberry ice-cream on the upper part of the lettering.
6. Drop vanilla ice-cream on the cone.
7. Drop vanilla ice-cream on floor for post work.
8. Finalize the artwork after photographing and retouching.

Arqueolític

Designer   Miquel Amela, Ferran Rodríguez
Design Agency   Enserio
Client   Arqueolític

This project is a brochure for Arqueolític, a company that offers a variety of scientific services and opportunities to discover our past in an experimental way through interpretation, experimentation and manipulation. For this project, the designers built stamps with erasers that were used to finish the pieces.

1	2	4a	4b
3a	3b	5a	5b

Materials & tools

erasers, template, cutter, glue, wooden base

Process

1. Design and print the letters "Arqueolític" and get the erasers ready.

2. Cut the letters to create the template. Mark the form above the eraser.

3. Cut the letters on the erasers with the cutter.

4. Hook the erasers above the wooden base.

5. Use as a stamp, paint and press it on a piece of paper.

ARQUEOLÍTIC

Serveis i propostes didàctiques de ciències socials
Estudi i difusió de patrimoni

Arqueolític neix a l'any 1992 per dur a terme propostes pel coneixement del nostre patrimoni i les ciències socials adaptades per a diferents públics. El nostre treball es basa en l'experimentació, la interpretació i la manipulació per tal de fer reviure el nostre passat. La nostra tasca professional es desenvolupa en tota la geografia del Principat i els nostres beneficiaris són molt diversos: museus, escoles, instituts, associacions, universitats, institucions, parcs arqueològics, cases de colònies, parcs naturals...

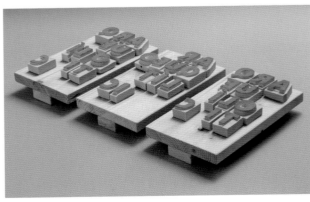

Arial Family

Designer   Alex Palazzi, Eudald Carré, Mio Ouchi

Arial family is an experimental project, it is an exploration of the human body changes based on a typographic family. The Arial font is explored using the evolution of a human body, and it is a relationship between typography and human flesh that changes in the font weight.

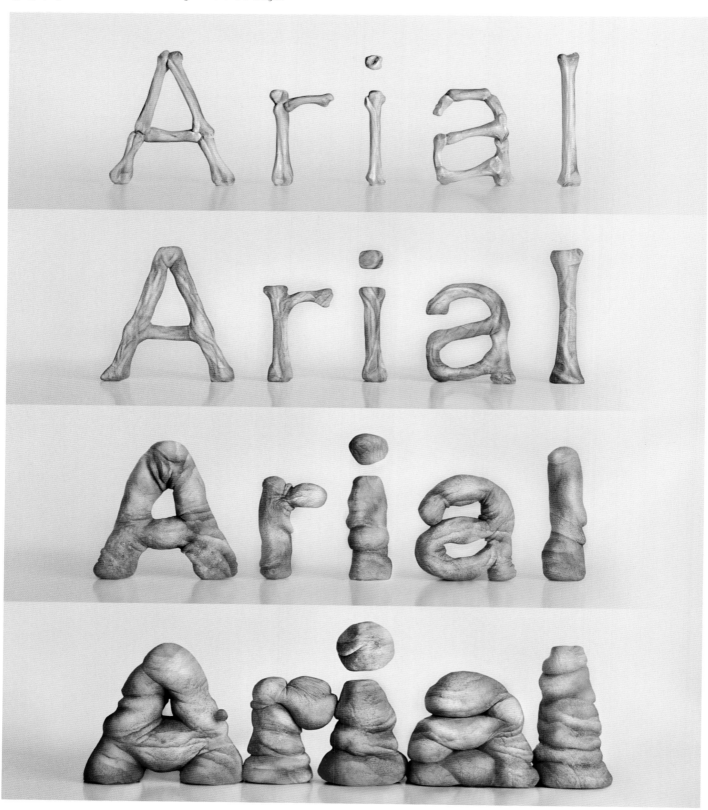

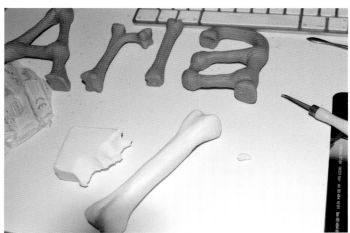

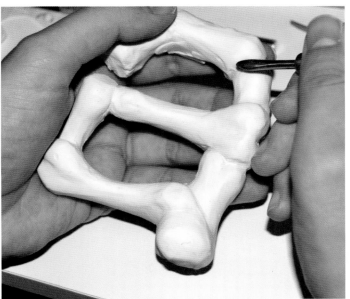

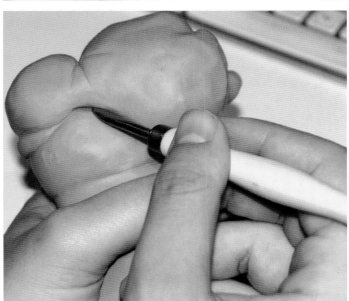

		1	2
	4	3a	3b
		3c	

Materials & tools

clay, sculpting tools, camara, digital programs

Process

1. Choose the font family Arial.

2. Make the models of the Arial family in the different weights: light, regular, bold, black.

3. Work on the details of each letter.

4. Shoot photos of all fonts and retouch them.

Always Create a Piece of Heart

Designer   Peter Kortleve   *Client*   Graphic Design Festival Breda (NL)
Design Agency   Shortlife Graphic Design

In a story about art it said that it's not just the object you're buying. The artist has put
his heart and soul into every aspect of it. So, you're not just buying a piece of art, you're
buying a piece of heart. This inspired the designer to create his motto "Always Create a
Piece of Heart." The green color stands for the color of money (greed), which is not what
you should be thinking of when you're creating something new.

Materials & tools

inkpad, heartshaped stamp, lightpad, scanner, computer

Process

1. Design the typography and the stamp.

2. Create the typography with the inkpad and heartshaped stamp, using a lightpad.

3. Scan and retouch the stamped artwork to finish the poster.

		1
	2a	3
	2b	

Medialab Exhibitor System

Design Agency   PKMN Architectures
Client   Medialab Prado Madrid

The Medialab Exhibitor System consisted of a flexible and re-arrangeable structure for exhibition purposes to be used by Medialab institution in Madrid, to show ongoing projects. The work concerning lettering was about naming the projects of a specific exhibition called "Ojo al Data."

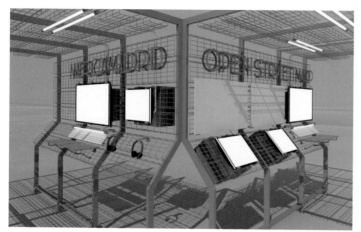

1	2a	
2b	3a	3c
3b		

Materials & tools

methacrylate, screwing and threaded rod, CNC machine

Process

1. Render the lettering system in the digital programs.

2. Use the methacrylate in green and grey colours to form the letters and cut by means of a CNC machine.

3. Mount the letters by using screws and threaded rods, and complete the entrance sign.

Orangerie

Design Agency   PKMN Architectures
Client   The Orangerie

The project was about a big scale sign to be installed at the entrance of a kindergarden in a small city in the centre-west of France called Niort. The purpose was to give the building an identity associated with its name and the colour suggested by the name. An additional goal was to get a functional arrangement of this sign so that it could be used by parents to sit and wait at the entrance of the building.

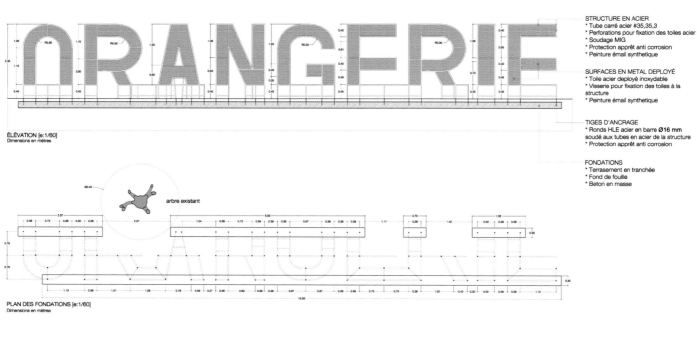

STRUCTURE EN ACIER
* Tube carré acier #35,35,3
* Perforations pour fixation des toiles acier
* Soudage MIG
* Protection apprêt anti corrosion
* Peinture émail synthetique

SURFACES EN METAL DEPLOYÉ
* Tole acier deployé inoxydable
* Visserie pour fixation des toiles à la structure
* Peinture émail synthetique

TIGES D'ANCRAGE
* Ronds HLE acier en barre Ø16 mm soudé aux tubes en acier de la structure
* Protection apprêt anti corrosion

FONDATIONS
* Terrasement en tranchée
* Fond de fouille
* Beton en masse

ÉLÉVATION [e:1/60]
Dimensions en mètres

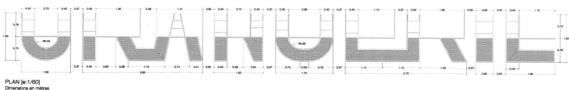

arbre existant

PLAN DES FONDATIONS [e:1/60]
Dimensions en mètres

PLAN [e:1/60]
Dimensions en mètres

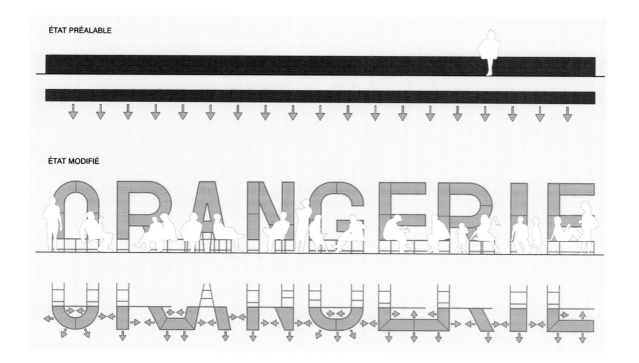

ÉTAT PRÉALABLE

ÉTAT MODIFIÉ

1a	1c	2
	3	
1b	4	

Materials & tools

metal, nails, mesh, orange paint

Process

1. Arrange the plans for the letters and render them.

2. Make small models of the letters using metal, nails, and mesh.

3. Paint the small models in an orange color.

4. Make the models in real size and install the letters.

Side vs Side — Work Hard Laugh Harder

Designer   Oliver Booth, Dave Greasley
Design Agency   Side by Side

After one year's work commissioned by clients, the designers came up with a large internal project called "Side vs Side." As part of the whole project, this piece was the answer to the question "What is the most important thing you have learned in the last year?" hand carved from breeze blocks. The "laugh harder" was reversed out from the carved waste.

Materials & tools

breeze blocks, hammer, chisels, coarse sandpaper

Process

1. Draw the wording onto each breeze block with chalk.
2. Make a rough outline using a hammer and chisel.
3. Chisel away the waste.
4. Use the coarse sandpaper to smooth rough areas.
5. Collect the waste for setting up the shoot, where "laugh harder" was reversed out.

1	2	
3	4	5

VIDA

Designer   Camilo Rojas
Design Agency   CR-eate

The project VIDA is created by Camilo Rojas in collaboration with Vlopz. After conceptualizing, sketching and designing, they carried out brainstorming and research on materials to execute the piece. Using 950 syringes and needles on the board, the final piece is 24" x 48" in size.

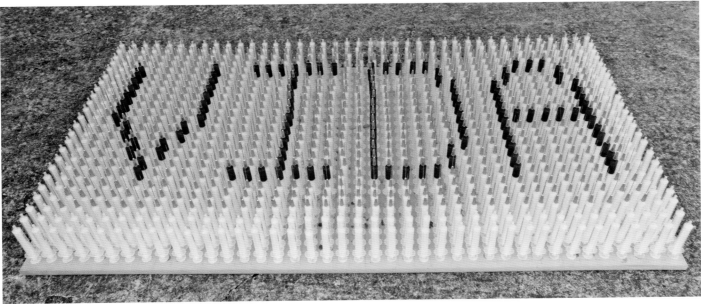

Materials & tools

syringes, needles, pigment, plywood, glue

Process

1. Draw a perfectly aligned grid on the plywood surface where the syringes will be pasted.

2. Create a pigment with the exact color of blood using a real blood sample from a butcher shop and fill the syringes with the pigment.

3. Paste over 950 syringes on the plywood without the needles.

4. Carefully attach sharp needles on the syringes.

5. Completed final piece.

1	2	4
3a		
3b		5

Ultimaker 3D Typography

Designer Freek Stortelder   *Client* Ultimaker
Design Agency Studio Daad

This piece of 3D typography is designed for Ultimaker, who creates 3D printers which are easy for everyone to use. In their communication, Ultimaker uses really powerful quotes. The challenge was to design those quotes into a playful and creative visual, to inspire architects, designers and engineers.

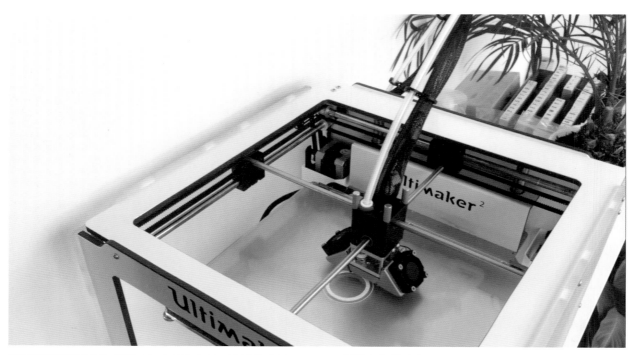

1		3	4a
2a			
2b		4b	

Materials & tools

Illustrator, 3D printer, glue, paint, camera

Process

1. Create the artwork "6" in Illustrator.

2. Print the elements and paint them.

3. Assemble the elements.

4. Photograph for the final image.

Swarovski Typography

Art Director	Matthew Knapp		*Client*	New York Lottery
Designer	Camilo Rojas		*Photographer*	Alain Almiñana
Design Agency	CR-eate		*Advertising Agency*	DDB, New York, USA

This project is a commissioned typographic installation of three tag lines and 83 letters staggered with over 36,000 Swarovski crystals, to be used in printed ads running on buses, shelters and subway stations in New York! Brainstorm, research, and sketching were carried out before the execution.

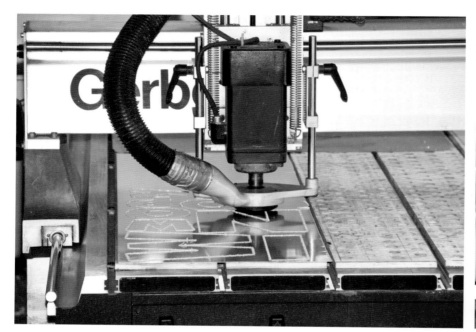

Materials & tools

paper, sheet metal, laser cutter, tweezers, Swarovski crystals, camera

Process

1. Following the outline of each letter, lasercut them on sheet metal to create perfect letters.
2. With the tweezers, carefully paste the Swarovski crystals on the surface of each letter.
3. Align all the taglines.

1a	1b	3a
2a	2b	3b

Photograph each of the phrases and retouch them in the computer.

Sainsbury's Twist Your Favourites
— Food Typography

Designer	Oliver Booth, Dave Greasley	Client	Sainsbury's
Design Agency	Side by Side		(via AnalogFolk)

UK-based design studio Side by Side was asked by AnalogFolk to create
six bespoke food typography pieces as part of a campaign called "Twist Your
Favourites" for Sainsbury's, a local supermarket retailer.

Each piece uses the main ingredient for the "twisted recipe": coffee, chorizo,
anchovies, horseradish, honey, and dark chocolate. This project is about
the type made from dark chocolate: shards/grated for "dark" and melted for
"chocolate," on a distressed wooden background.

		4	
1	2	3a	3b

Materials & tools

dark chocolate, blow torch, knives, graters, squeeze bottles

Process

1. With the blow torch, prepare the background following the initial sketch.

2. Prepare the dark chocolate using knives and graters.

3. Create the lettering.

4. Light and photograph the final image.

Ruim

- -

Designer   Marloes van Dijk   *Client*   Ruim Den Bosch
Design Agency   Studio Daad

- -

Ruim (spacious, broad) is a group of young entrepreneurs with a passion for creating a better socioeconomic environment. Ruim wants to create a vibrant city where learning, creation, and sharing come together. To create a 3D logo for Ruim to represent the client's innovative and enterprising way of work, Studio Daad handcrafted the typography, using black and white paper and wood.

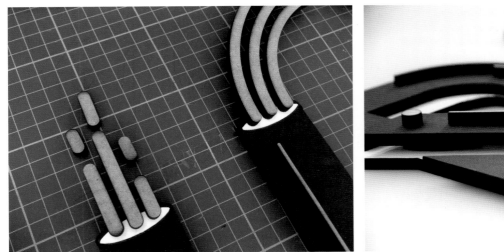

Materials & tools

pen, paper, wood, laser cutter

Process

1. Start the design process by hand drawing the letterforms and illustrations in and around the letters.

2. Laser cut the typography and illustrations and assemble the elements.

3. Use black and white paper.

4. Create different layers to realize the 3D logo.

1a	1b	3	4a
2		4b	

Reflexió

Concept & Art Director   Ramon Carreté   *Photographer*   Carles Guinot
Graphic Designer   José Alcázar, Núria Galí, Carles Carreté

The project uses magic and visual contradiction to transition from digital language to analog world. The construction of letters on a mirror creates new realities through reflection, which are neither truth nor falsehood.

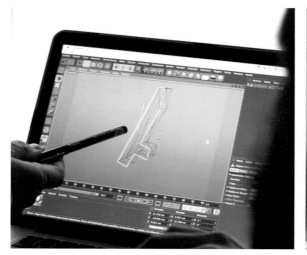
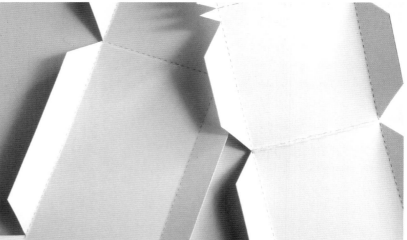

1	2a	2c	3
			4
2b		5	

Materials & tools

paper, mirror, paper cement, camera

Process

1. Drawing of letters. Creation of 3D models cut by one of its symmetry axis.

2. Printing and cutting. This step includes creasing the paper and cutting the flaps.

3. Gluing. To build the letters, paper cement was used.

4. Sticking. Placement of the letters on the mirror using a level.

5. Taking photographs.

For more details about the making-of, please visit www.vimeo.com/117475191.

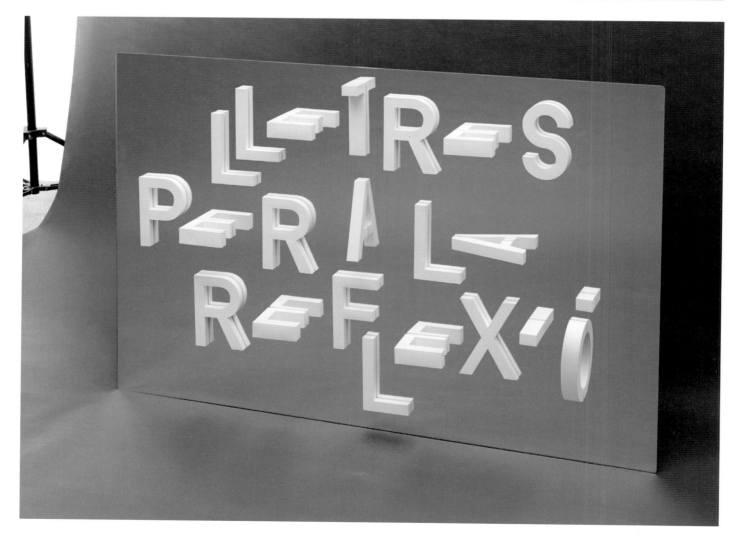

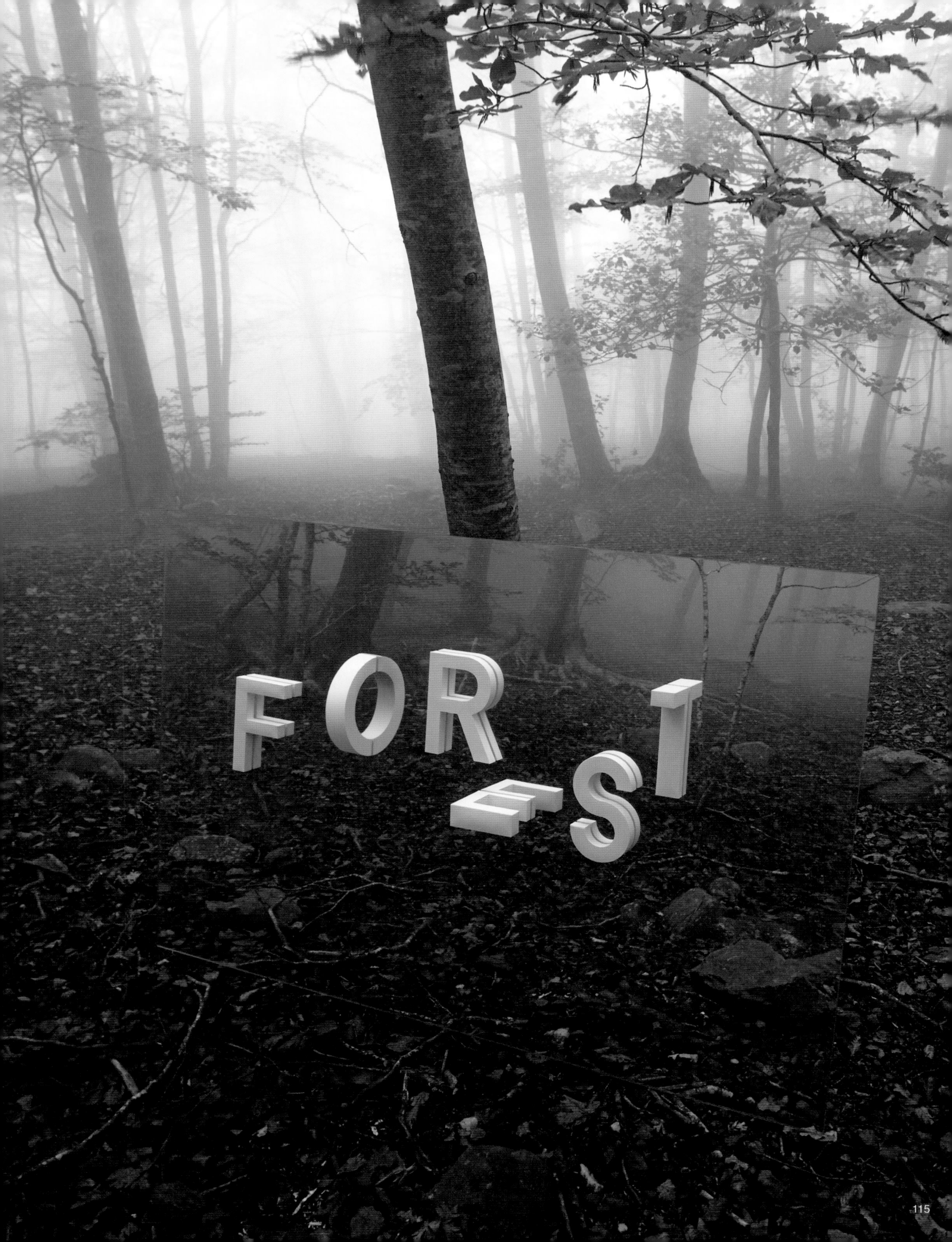
FOREST

Posi+ivo

- -
Designer   Camilo Rojas
Design Agency   CR-eate
- -

Posi+ivo was created to target mainly young people and create awareness about the worldwide issue of STDs. This project was showcased in the traveling exhibit MTV Teen Age Clicks which explores the behavior and habits of today's youth.

More than 2,800 condoms were placed on a 22"x90" canvas. The black condoms, which surround the word "positive," represent death and the negative aspects of this issue. The red condoms, which spell the word "positive," represent love, help, blood and the positive aspect of the problem.

Materials & tools

condoms, paper, canvas, glue, computer, camera

Process

1. Conceptualize, sketch and design the word "posi+ivo" in computer.

2. Research the materials and get the condoms ready to execute the piece.

3. Outline the created typography on canvas and carefully paste the condoms on the canvas.

4. The final completed piece.

1	2	3b	3c
3a		4	

Patience & Discipline

Designer   Xavier Casalta, Rémy Boiré

"Patience & Discipline" is a collaborated illustration and typography project. The pointillism is done by Xavier Casalta with the stippling technique and the line work is by Rémy Boiré, using Rotring inkpens and millions of handmade dots and lines.

4		2b	2c
		3a	3b
1	2a	3c	

Materials & tools

paper, Rotring inkpen, ink

Processw

1. Draw the outline of the letters "Patience & Discipline."
2. Add the surrounding decorations.
3. Fill in the letters and decorations with the Rotring inkpens.
4. Work on the details to realize the final piece.

Oranjebitter Festival

Design Agency   Mals
Client   Oranjebitter Festival / BPL Events

The Oranjebitter Festival logo holds an image of granny's old floor lamp, to represent the festival's good feeling. For their lucky 7th anniversary, the studio Mals thought it would be best to upgrade that lamp a little bit and give it some more power. It took over 600 light bulbs, 120 meters of cable light and 200 meters of wiring to create this tower of light by hand.

121

Materials & tools

wood, metal, paint, power tool, wire, light bulb

Process

1. Decide the colors and type to use, then sketch it out in Adobe Illustrator.
2. Draw the blueprint onto the wood.
3. Use power tools to cut out the pieces.
4. Hand tools are used to cut the metal into strips, and then nailed onto the wood.
5. Holes are drilled for the light bulbs, and the signs are ready for paint.
6. The signs are painted with spray paint and left to dry for the night.
7. The light bulbs are installed and soldered.
8. More wiring and connecting all the electronics together.
9. Install all the signs to the frame, making a tower of signs.
10. Connect all the wires and check for the last time.

1	2	7	
3	4	8	9
5	6		10

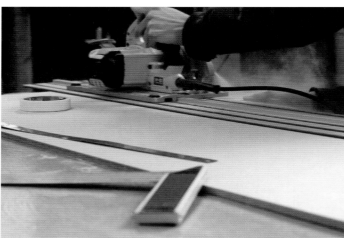
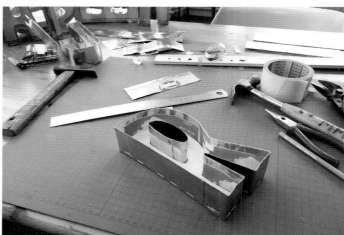

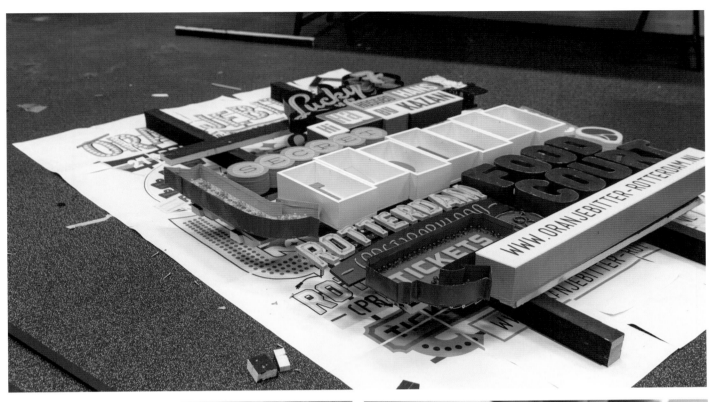

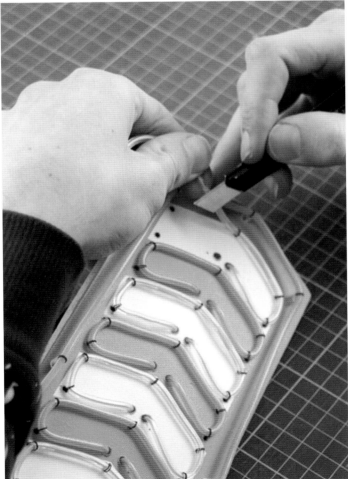

Malmö Festival

Design Agency Snask
Client City of Malmö

This project is the world's largest identity for Scandinavia's largest city festival. To help Malmö festival celebrate in style, the studio Snask created the largest physical graphic identity: a gigantic physical art installation measuring 13×8 meters. The installation was interaction-friendly and visitors could jump, climb, or just plain chill on it. To produce this masterpiece they used 10,000 nails, 175 liters of paint, 280 plywood sheets and 14 people during 900 hours. A sky lift was rented to photograph it 30 meters up in the air.

1a		3a
1b	2a	
	2b	3b

Materials & tools

nails, paint, plywood sheet

Process

1. Create the letters and shapes following the initial sketch.

2. Transport them and put them together on site.

3. Photograph for digitalization.

IL — Intelligence in Lifestyle Magazine

Art Director   Francesco Franchi
Craftwork   Andrea Manzati
Design Agency   Happycentro

Designer & Lettering   Federico Galvani
Client   Intelligence in Lifestyle Magazine

This project is created collaborating with IL — Intelligence in Lifestyle Magazine, supplement of Il Sole 24 Ore. Under the creative direction of Mr. Francesco Franchi, each month they developed the title typography using different techniques and materials for the brand new column "Remo Contro" written by the Italian philosopher Remo Bodei.

Materials & tools

paper, tissue, thread, plasticine

Real illustrations, made with pencil sketches and thin black pen, for "Legalità."

Vectorial illustration and plotter for "Rischio."

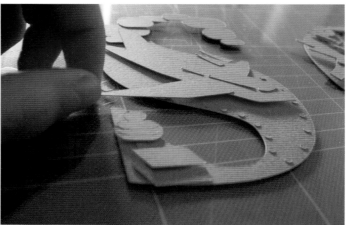

Tissues and threads, and hand cut for "Povertà."

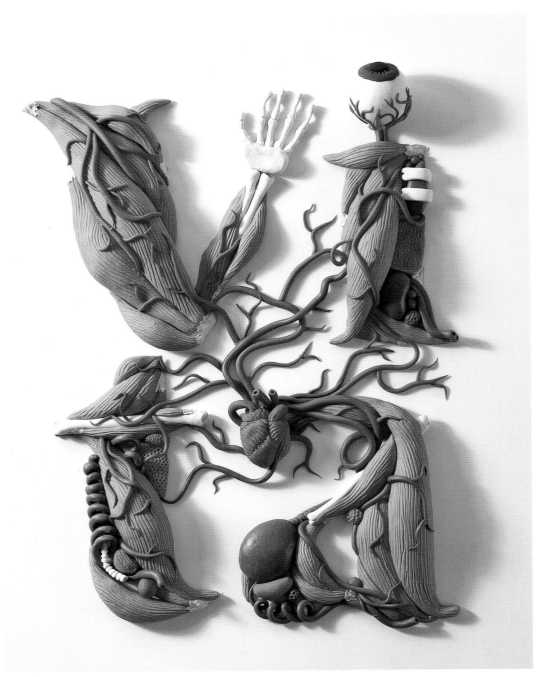

Vectorial illustration and plotter for "Curiosità."

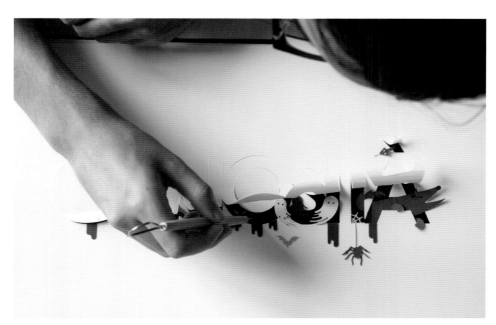

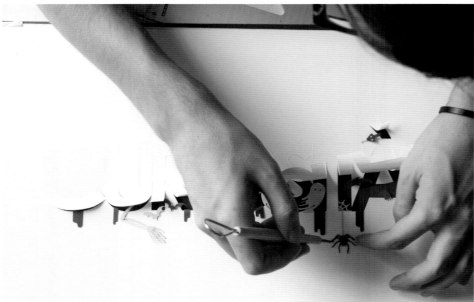

Sketchup 3D modeling and paper cut and fold for "Identità."

H — 36 Days of Type

Designer & Illustrator Anna Oro, Anna Rodighiero
Design Agency Happycentro
Laser Cut Fablab Verona

Photographer Federico Padovani
Client 36 Days of Type

36 Days of Type began when Barcelona-based graphic designers Nina Sans and Rafa Goicoechea first decided to challenge themselves and a few colleagues to design one letter each day and post them on their Instagram feed, setting daily personal design challenges and experimenting with new approaches.

The main inspiration to create the project came when Victor Bregante suggested the idea of making this exercise globally and simultaneously, and the result is the design of a capital "H." This is a project that aims to create a space for creation around typography and its endless graphic possibilities.

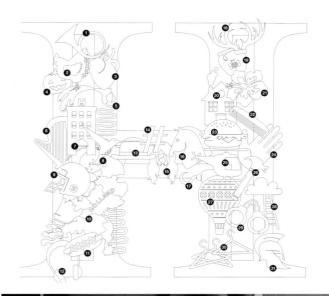

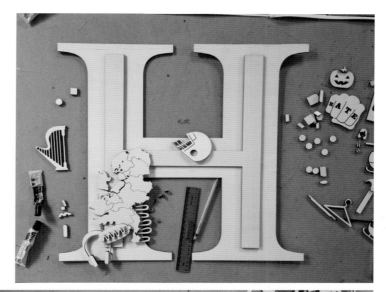

Materials & tools

Adobe Illustrator, paper, glue, wood

Process

1. Initial digital sketch.

2. The word "H" and all the details were laser cut.

3. Glue all the details to H following the printed sketch.

Forest Gothic Typeface Lettering

Artist Ciprian Udrescu

As an artist who usually draws and paints, Ciprian took inspiration from everything around him. Typography and lettering is something he always loves to do. Inspired by an old writing style from an old book, this typeface is related to that kind of imagery, of copperplate engraving and Albrecht Durer`s engraving. The walnut ink is used for these types because it is very fluid and enables the artist to draw very organic lines and shapes.

Materials & tools

walnut ink, dip pen, pencil, paper

Process

1. Research and plan the typeface.

2. Draw the basic forms of the letters with the pencil.

3. Add the very organic lines and shapes like leaves and twisted wood branches to the letters with a pen and walnut ink.

4. Work on the details to complete the final image.

4b	1	2
	3a	3b
4c	4a	

136

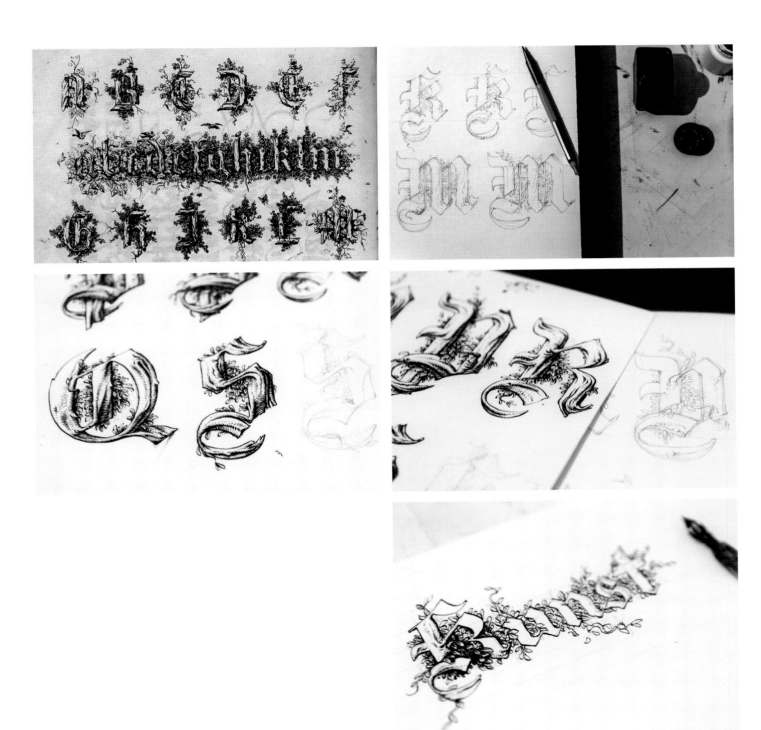

Flavor

- -
Designer   Camilo Rojas
Design Agency   CR-eate
- -

Flavor is part of an installation series created to expose audiences to a particular idea through the power of typography and demonstrate how it could communicate and represent outside of the usual screen and print based forms. This piece was created using over 3,400 cigarettes. The cigarettes spelling the word "Flavor" are half smoked showing the nicotine in them.

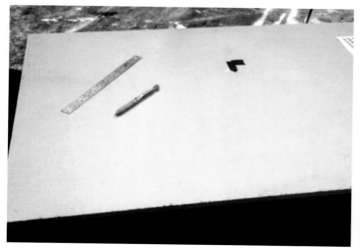

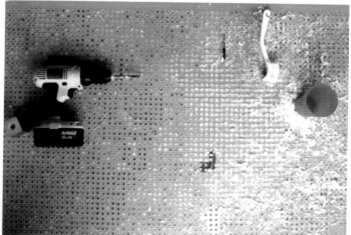

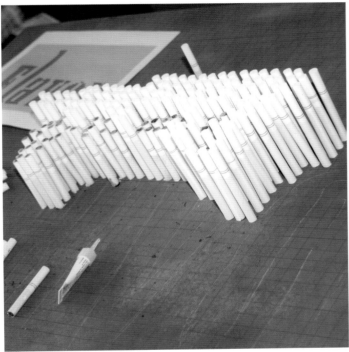

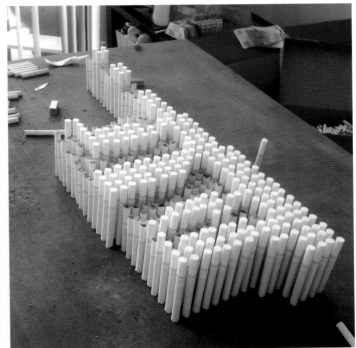

4c	3a	3b
1	2	4a	4b

Materials & tools

pencil, ruler, drill, acrylic board, cigarettes, paper

Process

1. Draw a perfectly aligned grid on the acrylic board with a ruler and pencil.

2. Drill each hole carefully on the acrylic board surface.

3. "Smoke" (or technically extract) the nicotine of each cigarette.

4. Paste over 3,000 cigarettes on the acrylic board surface.

Festimal

Designer   Freek Stortelder   *Client*   Afdeling Apps
Design Agency   Studio Daad

This project is the design for a splashscreen for a festimal app. It is created to appeal to festival organizers. The typography is elaborated with elements found at most festivals, like music, lighting and tasty drinks. The letters are dancing around, creating a dynamic and enthusiastic image.

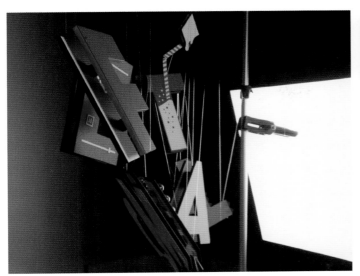

Materials & tools

wood, paper, lasercutter, camera, Illustrator, lighting

1	2	4	5a
3		5b	

Process

1. Decide which colors to use to create a very enthusiastic image and start by lasercutting the typography.

2. Create the letters by using two layers for an awesome 3D look.

3. Provide the wooden letters with colored paper, illustrations and lights.

4. Create a hanging system to make the letters dynamic.

5. Photograph the type in a studio.

Eye Candy

- -

Designer   Patrick Simons
Design Agency   Van Honing

- -

Eye Candy is a personal experiment to explore the possibilities of handmade typography. Hundreds and thousands of colorful candies were used to emphasize the diversity of the Helvetica.

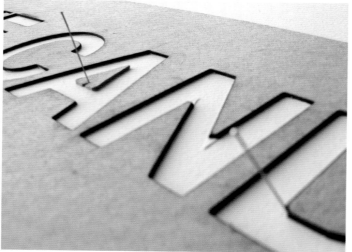

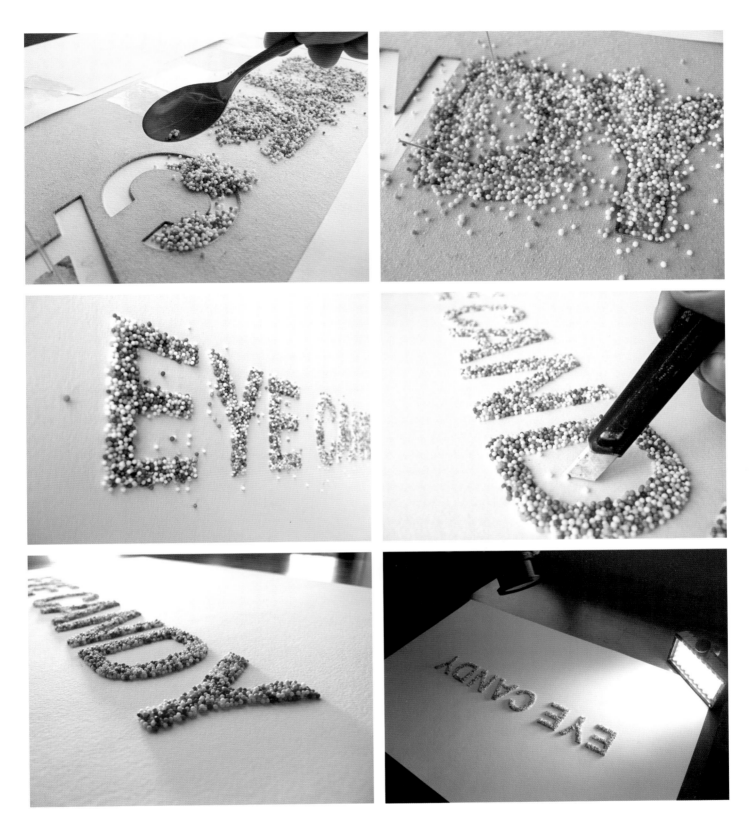

Materials & tools

grey board carton, candies, laser cutter, light, camera

Process

1. Laser cut the letters on a piece of grey board carton following the sketch.

2. Fill the letters with colorful candies.

3. Carefully remove the candies scattered around the letters.

4. Prepare the light to shoot the final image.

4b		2b	2c
		3a	3b
1	2a	3c	4a

EUCD Tex10

Designer	Juan Pablo Sabini, Matías Fiori
Design Agency	Re-robot Studio
Client	EUCD (Escuela Centro de Diseño)

For some years now, students of the Bachelor's Degree in Textile Design have been carrying out an end-of-year event including the collections they have designed for the course. Commissioned by EUCD, Re-robot studio created the identity design including naming, poster, printed catalog, web, and invitations among other pieces. The team generated a large woven paper piece, upon which they created typography with the name conceived for this generation "tex10", in a direct and euphonic manner. The layout and design of the remaining work were developed from this woven piece, using the same concept of orthogonal organization. The catalog's interior layout stands on the idea of diversity and each double page is different from the next, whilst maintaining the same aesthetic coherence.

Helvetica Neue LT Std 97

hamburgefontsiv
AaBbCc

Quiroga Serif Pro*

hamburgefontsiv

hamburgefontsiv

hamburgefontsiv

Aa**Bb***Cc*

C: 16	C: 56
M: 100	M: 7
Y: 96	Y: 0
K: 2	K: 0

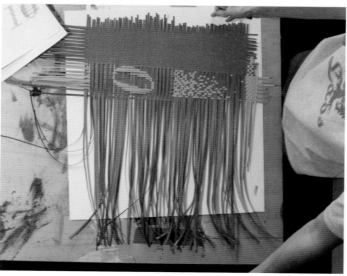

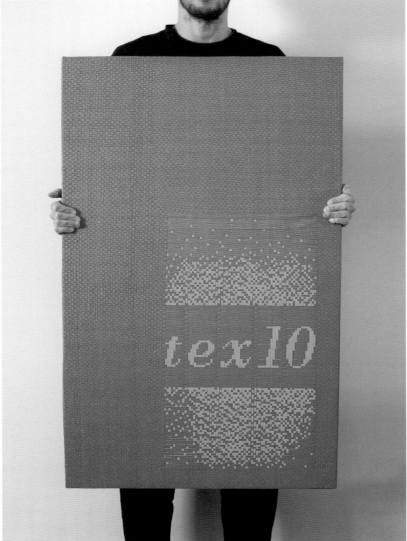

1a		3a
1b	2a	
2b	2c	3b

Materials & tools

weaving materials

Process

1. Decide the palette. Design the letters "tex10" and prepare the materials.

2. Print the letters, then weave the letters using weaving materials of different colors.

3. Complete the whole piece and take photos.

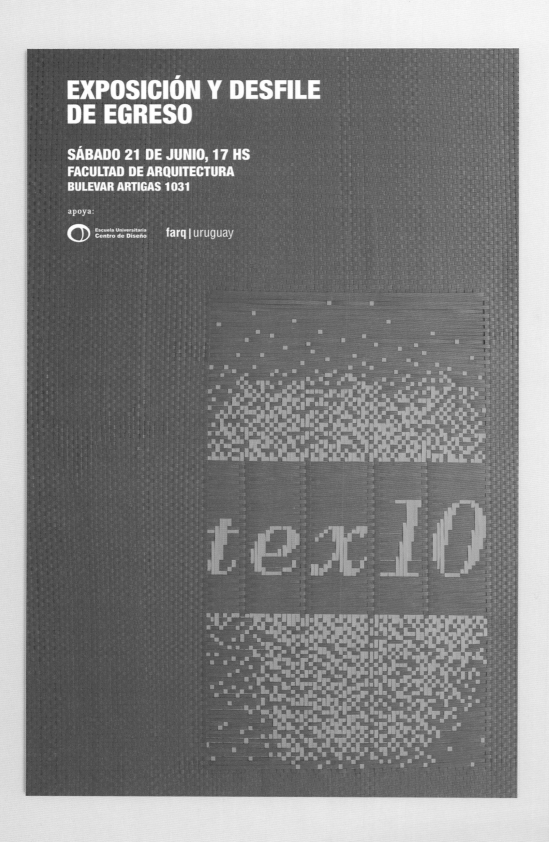

EXPOSICIÓN Y DESFILE
DE EGRESO

SÁBADO 21 DE JUNIO, 17 HS
FACULTAD DE ARQUITECTURA
BULEVAR ARTIGAS 1031

apoya:

Escuela Universitaria
Centro de Diseño

farq | uruguay

tex10

NIGHT
LIGHTS
NATALIA TRONCOSO

Colección de indumentaria & Alta Costura inspirada en el Hotel Casino Carrasco y en la Kinesfera.

Se toma como punto de partida la elegancia simbólica del edificio en la sociedad montevideana y se conjuga con los conceptos de movimiento y proyección de los mismis empleados en la kinesfera.

Fotografía / Postproducción: Bruno Noguerra • Maquillaje / Pelo: Amapola Vera • Modelo(s): Natalia Sada, Natalia Cuarpa y Valentina Carbonell • Asistente(s): Valentina Carbonell • Calzado: Datelli • Contacto: nat1210bl@gmail.com

De Ondergrondse

Designer   Freek Stortelder   *Client*   Jasper van Rosmalen

Design Agency   Studio Daad

De Ondergrondse is an underground techno party held in awesome basements. For this event, Studio Daad designed the identity, consisting of logo, posters, flyers, stickers and a teaser. The 3D blocks symbolize the city in which De Ondergrondse is literally underground. When the set starts, it will be felt throughout the city.

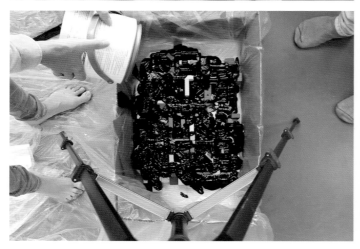

1a		3a
1b	2b	
2a		3b

Materials & tools

wooden blocks, paint, pigment powder, glue, brush

Process

1. Start with some blocks and a typographic sketch. The negative space became the most important and resulted in a readable design. Connect every single piece together with glue. The result is a typographic construction.

2. With a brush, hand-paint the entire construction pitch black.

3. Fill the construction with yellow pigment powder and place it on a huge sound speaker. While playing some underground techno beats underneath the work, the bass starts to create the artwork.

DASHAPE

Designer   Andrés Momó, Jaime García
Design Agency Olé Studio

Client DASHAPE

DASHAPE is the biggest sneaker event in Spain. Olé Studio were responsible for the visual communication of this event. For the second edition, they came up with the idea of doing something handmade, avoiding the screen of the computer. Using the 'Futura Extra Bold Condensed ITC' type, they printed the letters and used them as a template, and then laced them. Each letter was made separately to have more versatility for the adaptations. The final image was retouched.

DA SHAPE

Sneaker Event

1	2	
3a	3b	5
3c	4	

Materials & tools

craft paper, awl, laces, Photoshop

Process

1. Sketch each letter and lay the craft paper underneath it.

2. Use the awl to drill holes and make sure that these holes go through the craft paper.

3. Thread the laces through the holes on the craft paper of each letter.

4. Take photos of the letters and import them into Photoshop for retouching.

5. Organize all digitalized letters together for the final image.

Cazuza — Visceral Solidarity: Time Doesn't Stop

Designer   Vitor Silva Paiva

The main theme of the project is the work of Brazilian singer and composer Cazuza. The artist's compositions are extraordinarily striking and strong. Phrases from his lyrics have become present in our routine. Based on this idea, the work consists of experimental graphic interpretations from the artist's phrases. A line of products, created from these interpretations for the NGO Viva Cazuza Society, were sold and the income retained.

Materials & tools

matchsticks, white glue, fire, camera, Photoshop

Process

1. Choice of material, element, and typography for the execution of the sentence.
2. Draft with pencil the phrase on paper, which is the basis for the collage of matchsticks.
3. Fixing of sticks with white glue forming the sentence.
4. Final assembly of the sentence in environments to photograph the action of fire.

1	2	3b	3c
3a		4	

Cazuza — Visceral Solidarity: Sincere Lies Interest Me

- -

Designer   Vitor Silva Paiva

- -

This project is related to illusion. It is based on wooden letters halved and then mirrored. Some letters were produced in half so that the mirror completes the original shape of the letter. So we have the mirror lie showing a nonexistent real world, as well as sincere lies.

1a	1b	2b	
		2c	2d
2a		2e	2f

Materials & tools

wood, spray, adhesive tape, mirror, camera, Photoshop

Process

1. Cut and finish the wooden letters and plan the letters with transparent tape.

2. Search for different places that bring more illusion, deceit and magic to the piece being photographed.

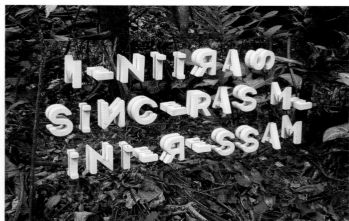

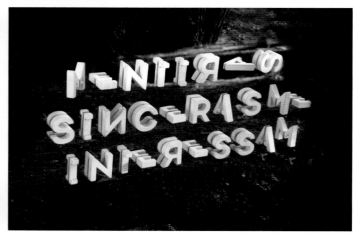

Typography for Popular Science

Designer Ruslan Khasanov
Client Popular Science Magazine

The premise of the story was that we could have found alien life, but it might be on the microscopic scale. According to the brief, the headline "have we found alien life" should have been in neon organic looking text on a dark background. The process of forming the letters was fascinating: how the empty, thin oil forms reveal ink drops of different colors that spread out across each form to fill the space, then merge to form stunning color combinations. This action is reminiscent of life.

Materials & tools

oil, water, ink, brush

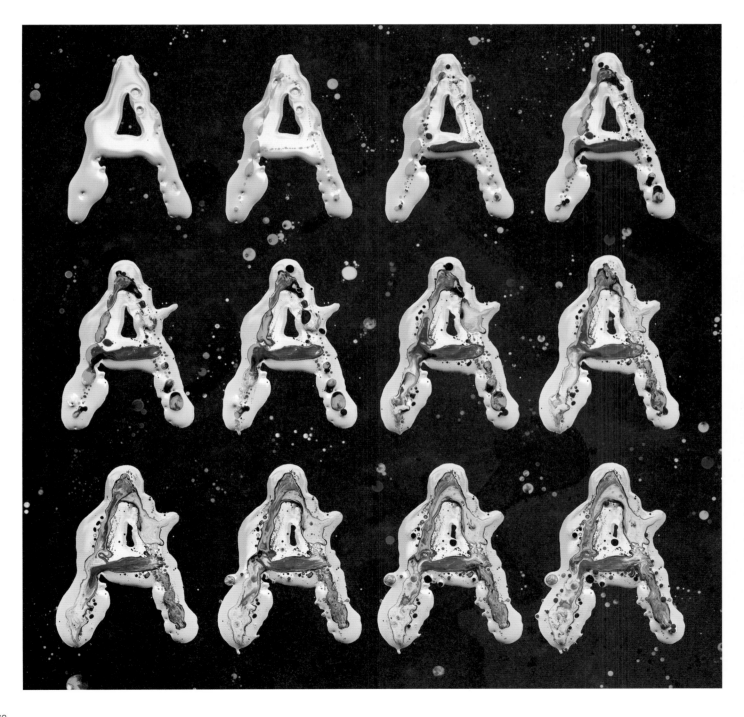

Sunbeam Type

Designer   Ruslan Khasanov

Sunbeam type was inspired by the light dispersion phenomenon, the splitting of the white light into a rainbow. To create this project, all the designer needed was to deflect the light by transparent refracting mediums. So he used a gel which was dabbed on a glass and then drew the letters on with a brush. Then he brought that glass to the sunbeam to reflect letters with a magnifying glass on the background.

Materials & tools

sunbeam, gel, glass, brush, magnifying glass

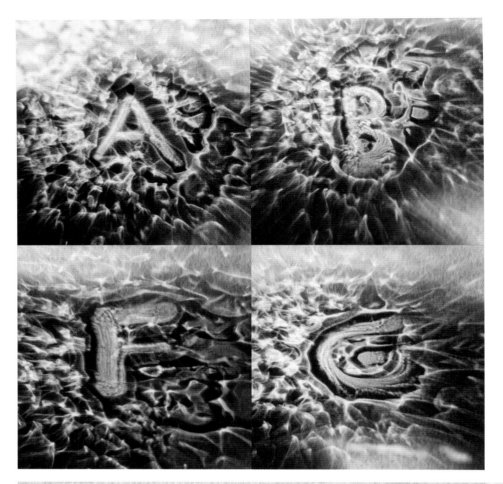

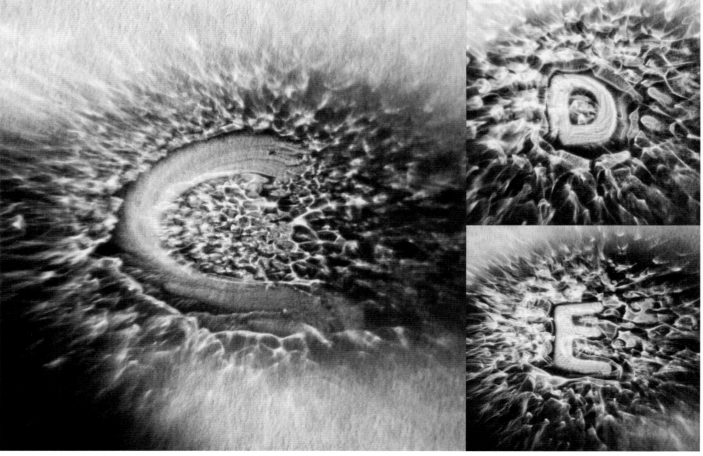

Sauce Type

Designer Ruslan Khasanov

This is a test graphic for a commission. Oil, water, and ink combine to create stunning and colorful spatial type. There is something cosmic in this graphic.

Materials & tools

oil, water, ink

Golden Liquid Type

Designer   Ruslan Khasanov

This project is a variation of the designer's liquid type, except that ink used here is gold paint too. The process of spreading paint on a damp surface is used again to create letters instantly overgrown with gold patterns that disappear when placed under a stream of water.

Materials & tools

water, gold paint, ink, brush

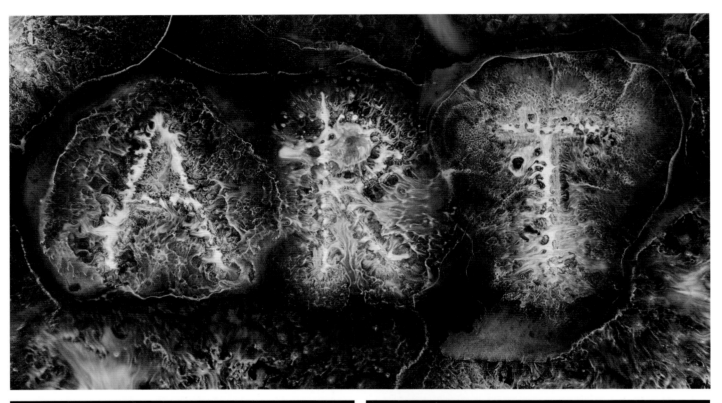

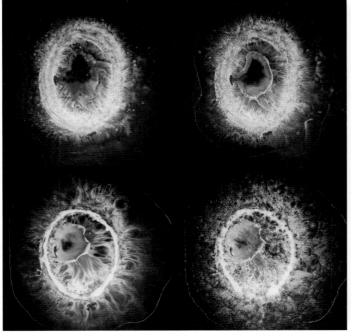

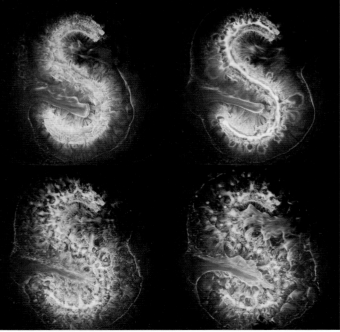

Lumen Type

Designer   Ruslan Khasanov

"Lumen Type" was born out of the blurry sight caused by not wearing glasses. Trials had been done in the dark. The designer used a syringe to leave droplets of water on a mirror surface in the shape of tiny letters, and then directed a flashlight on the forms from different angles and distances; and in the end, the bokeh and aberrations were brought out by a series of magnifying glasses.

Materials & tools

water, mirror, syringe, flashlight

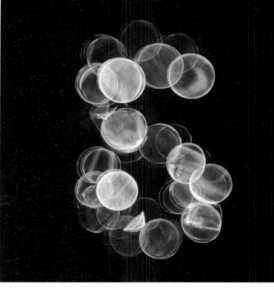
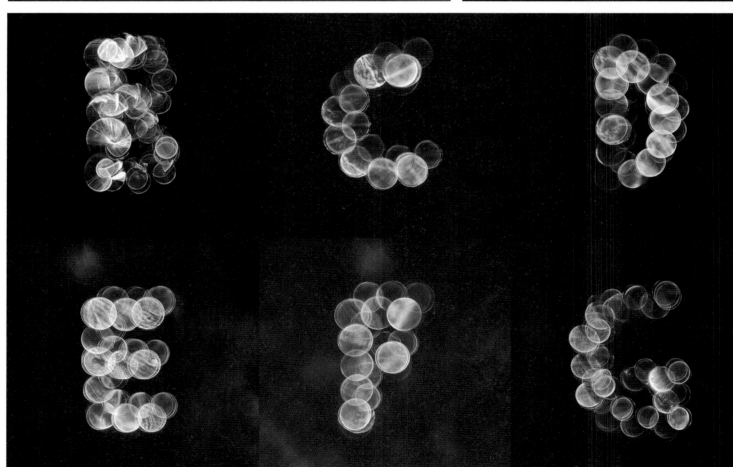

Cazuza — Visceral Solidarity: Brazil, Show Your Face

Designer   Vitor Silva Paiva

'Brazil, show your face' is an outburst all the existing problems in the country, so Brazil is masked. Not shown, it is hidden in several layers. Before execution, the designer carried out analysis of the best material for the context of the sentence and chose the best typography.

1	2	4b
	3	
4a		4c

Materials & tools

papers, stylus, pencil, camera, Photoshop

Process

1. Typography transferred to various papers through the carbon paper.

2. Cut out all the papers with a stylus.

3. Attach each paper to form several layers.

4. Photograph the piece and retouch it.

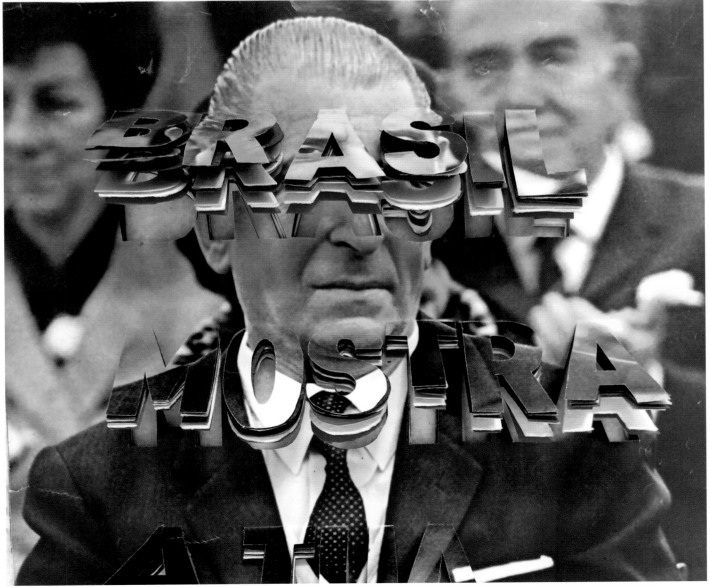

Bom Bom & Omali — Logos

Designer   Filipe Lizardo
Client   HBD

Two projects, one challenge.

The designer was invited by HBD to rethink and design a new hotel brand architecture, two projects located in the amazing island of São Tomé and Príncipe, Africa. The request was to create an artistic typeface that could transmit an eco-environment of sustainable guidance, community engagement, and natural heritage with a truly African inspiration. He began the process of drawing the identity using two usual natural elements: water and flour. It's all about simplicity, ancestral wisdom, harmony and freedom.

Materials & tools

valchromat black board, flour, water, brushes, hair-dryer, camera

Process

1. Select the valchromat black board and wheat flour.

2. Develop textures with brushes and uncommon markers (spoon, comb) to record and trace the body movements that define this crude, natural look of hand lettering.

3. Introduce water as the second element in Bom Bom to clear and sharpen the thin line of hand lettering and in Omali just reverse the process and use water as a marker and flour as a fixer. Create two distinct universes with the same main elements.

4. The photo shoot (making of) was used as a draft for the final digital output.

4	2b	3a
1	2a	3b

Good Vibes — Gratitude Wall

- -

Lettering, Designer & Art Director Camilo Rojas   *Photographer* Vlopz
Design Agency CR-eate

- -

It's inspiring. It's three-dimensional. It's alive. This Gratitude Wall is the main installation at CR-eate Studio. The 48 x 64 piece was created by combining typography and live moss.

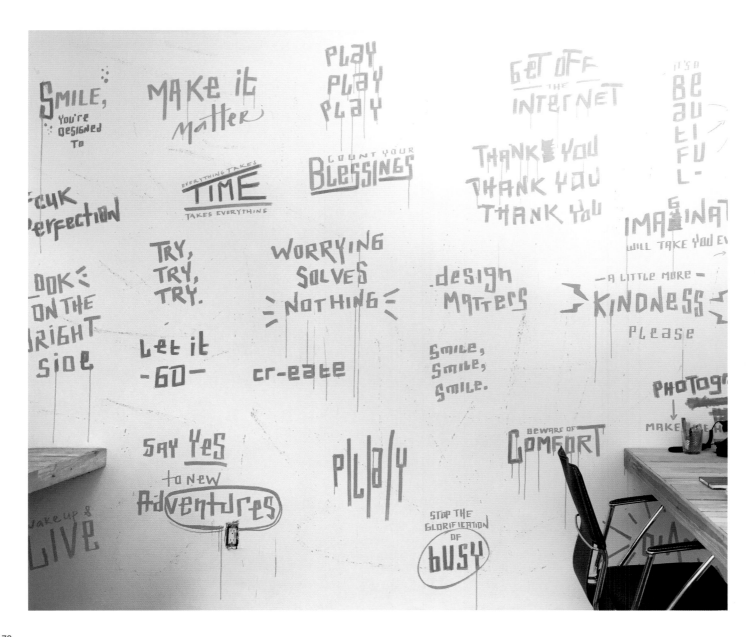

Materials & tools

pen, paper, acrylic, marker, laser cutter, spacers, live moss

Process

1. Motivational Words
   Gather sentences that motivate and best describe the work ethic. Using different styles
   of typography, give into the delicious dripping effect of the acrylic markers.

2. Good Vibes Sculpture
   a. Starting with pen and paper, scribble "Good Vibes."
   b. Connect all letters in order for it to be cut as one piece.
   c. Laser cut the letter piece, apply the wall spacers.
   d. Fill with living moss to make it come to life.
   e. Trim and water the sculpture routinely.

1a	1b	2a	2b	2c
1c		2d		2e

Attention: Craft

Design Agency   Snask
Client   Liljevalchs konsthall

This project is an identity for an summer exhibition of 2014 at one of Sweden's most respected galleries, Liljevalchs konsthall, where a range of magnificent craft artists and their works were presented. The graphic identity was made entirely out of crafted materials all wrapped in a minimalistic surrounding. The word CRAFT was designed through custom lettering and entirely handmade while the rest of the typography was kept simple and quiet. The production by hand and the choice of materials mirror the content of the exhibition without taking the attention away from the artists.

Materials & tools

copper, marble, porcelain, wood, stone

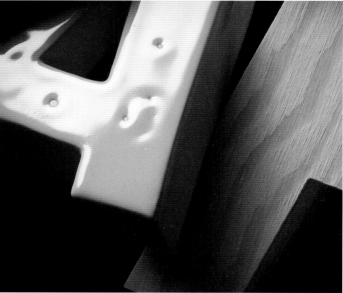

The Washington Post

Design Agency   Snask
Client   The Washington Post

This project is created for "The Favorites Issue" of
The Washington Post magazine, one of the biggest
newspapers in the U.S. The creative team Snask made
the cover and the editorial images entirely by hand.
They wanted to capture the essence of every category
in the design and illustration of each letter of the word
"Favorites" by creating fun, unique and physical icons
that would reflect the characteristics of each topic, all in
different materials.

Materials & tools

glass, plywood, concrete, neon light

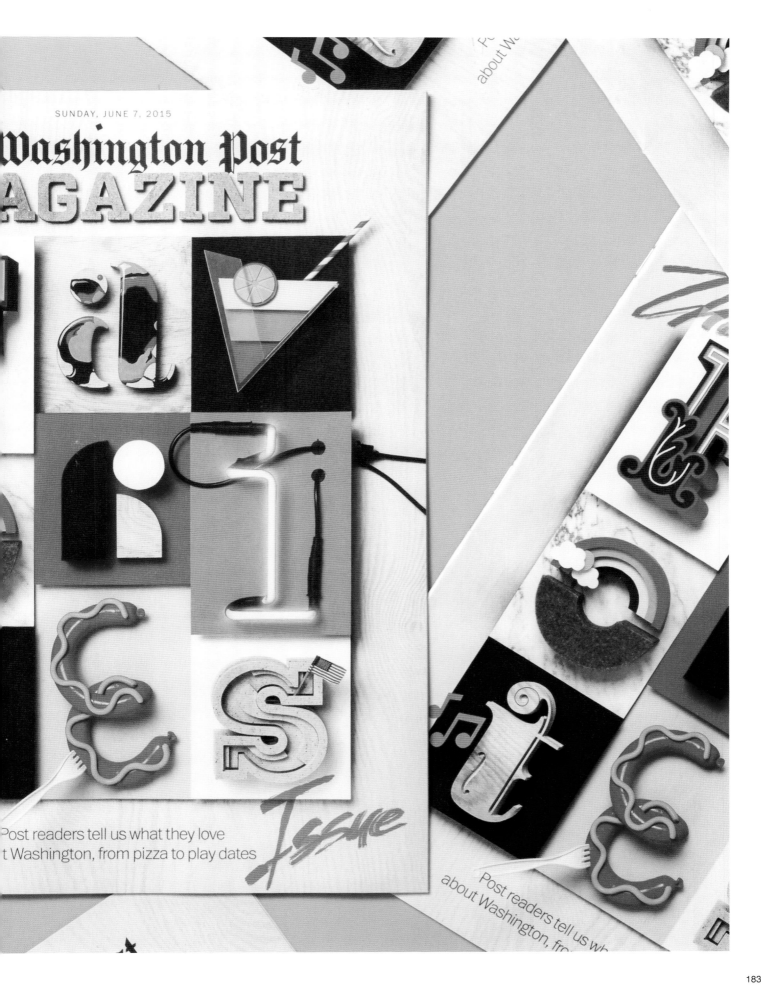

Watercolor Alphabet

Designer   Xavier Casalta

Fascinated by typographic compositions and illustrations with millions of handmade black dots, the designer wanted to experiment with something new, keeping that "dot" style in this project. It is a series of letters created with different bubbles of watercolor, using a syringe and watercolor on paper. The implementation went fast as the paper absorbs the watercolor bubbles.

Materials & tools

pen, paper, watercolor, syringe

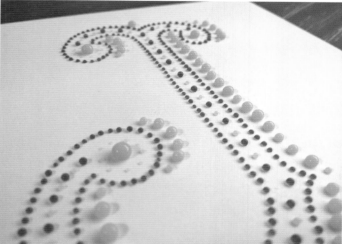

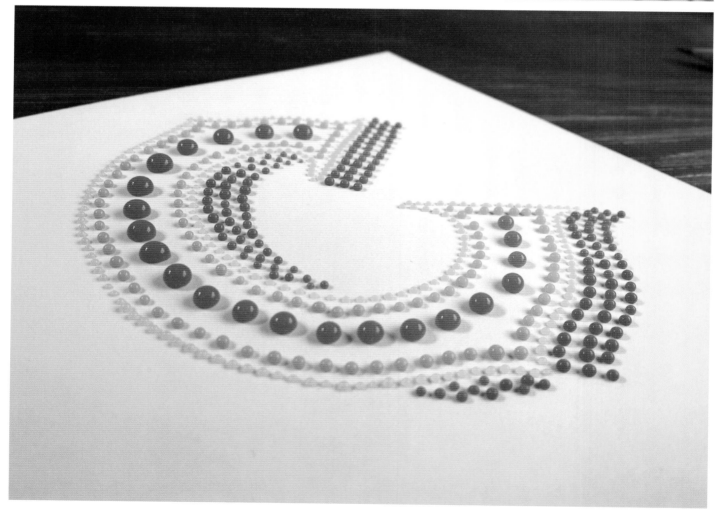

Printing Friends Magazine No.8 – Food

Design Agency   Snask
Client   DanagårdLiTHO

Printing Friends is a magazine about design and creativity which is published by the print house DanagårdLiTHO in Sweden. In 2014, the new Printing Friends opens up for new themes that appeal to a wider audience. In this issue No.8 – Food, Printing Friends took a culinary trip around the world and ate mashed potato typography, a coconut flavored "space burger" and a knitted hot dog among many other delicacies. So Snask handcrafted the Logo "P" for the cover in a way that related to the contents of the issue.

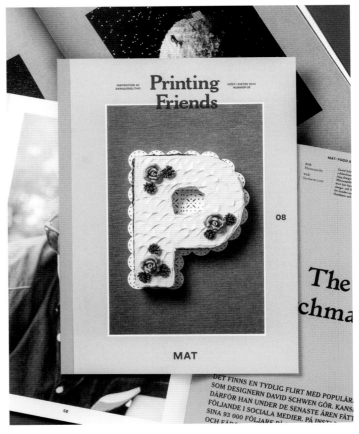

Work Hard Play Hard

Designer Scott Biersack
Client Zion & Zion

With Zion & Zion's newly built office, a large mural piece was wanted on the 2nd floor of the office, which is where their design and development team is located. As the CEO Aric likes to say, "Zion & Zion likes to work hard, and play hard." And of course, that was the perfect phrase to paint on the walls just before they held their Grand Opening party.

1	2	4a	4b
3		5	

Materials & tools

paper, pencil, color paint

Process

1. Initial concept sketches.

2. 2nd round of concept sketching.

3. Final proposed sketch to be painted on the wall.

4. Painting progress of the mural on the wall.

5. Finished piece and image with chairs shown for scale.

Wonders

Designer   Noelia Lozano
Client   Wonders

This project is a papercraft visual made by the designer for the spring/ summer campaign of Wonders Spanish brand shoes.

Materials & tools

paper, scissors, glue, scalpel, ruler, color papers, foam, cutting base

Process

1. Cut 1cm wide strips of the colors that will be used in the composition. You will need to sketch previously the lettering or illustration you want to develop on a program such as Illustrator or Photoshop.

2. Glue your sketch to a solid white base of foam, and start making the contour of the logo.

3. Use paper quilling tools to roll the strips of paper that are going to be inside the logo.

4. Continue filling all the holes inside the letters.

5. Finish the illustration by gluing the strips outside the lettering.

1	2	5a
3		
4		5b

Soup — Enjoy Your Own Composition of Taste!

Designer   Justyna Rzepa

Plasticine is a soft modeling material, used especially by children, but it also creates incredible opportunities for designers. The designer used this technique in this project to interesting effect. The poster has a mission of encouraging cooking and eating soups, and the saturated colors bring to mind the fresh and delicious taste of vegetables.

Materials & tools

plasticine, paper, pencil, chisel, camera, Adobe Photoshop

Process

1. Knead small pieces of plasticine to form the shapes of vegetables.

2. Sketch the inscription on a piece of paper. It was inspired by the shape of the AR CHRISTY font.

3. Form many simple shapes like long strips, balls and others by rolling plasticine in hands and press them on the paper's surface. Thanks to the mixing colors, more interesting effects become possible.

4. Use a sharp pencil to poke little dots and a chisel to create texture in some forms.

5. The biggest step was to fit small plasticine vegetables into relevant places in the artwork.

6. Add more shapes to finish the design.

1		6a
2	3	
4	5	6b

My Childhood

Designer   Alex Palazzi
Photographer of Godzilla   BFLV

"My Childhood" was done after a birthday when the designer realized that he was getting old. Since he was very young he had been fascinated by crafts. His generation experienced the transition from manual games to console games so he wanted this project to be a reflection of his way of working, a fusion between tactile and digital.

Materials & tools

rope, spin tops, clay, slime, plastic, sand toys, sculpting tools, camera

Process

1. Collect sand from the beach.

2. Put the castle on set after being covered with sand.

3. Paint rocks with gold spray.

4. Cover all the rocks.

5. Put the rocks in place.

6. Add elements.

7. Paint the cut wood letters with gold spray.

8. Position the letters in place after they were covered with sand.

9. Add toys.

1	2	7	
3	4		
5	6	8	9

Process

1. Draw the lettering on paper.
2. Prepare a clay surface with the same size as the paper where the lettering is drawn.
3. Cut the lettering following the same drawing lines.
4. Carve the lettering.
5. Prepare the spin tops.
6. Put the spin top rope in the same position as the drawing for the final photo shoot.
7. Photograph and retouch.

		3	
7		4	5
1	2	4	

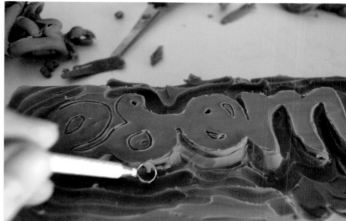
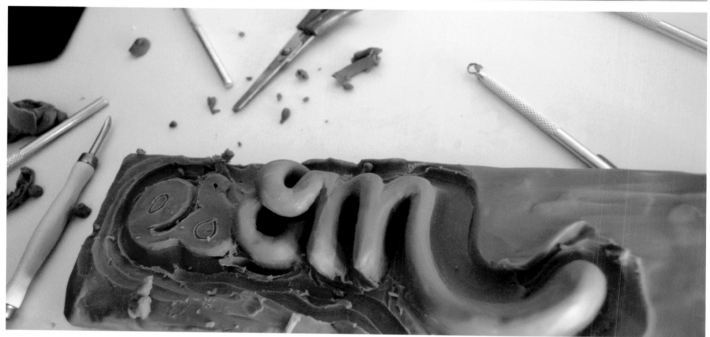

Process

1. Flat cut paper reference on top of a clay base.
2. Carve letters and add clay to letter volume.
3. Put the final letters on a stand.
4. Redefine the look.
5. Put slime on clean letters for dropping simulation.
6. Finalize the artwork through photographing and retouching.

1	2a	4	5a
2b			5b
2c	3	6	

Process

1. Vectorize letters.
2. Use cinema 4D to have a 3D reference image.
3. Photograph the gameboy with the same perspective as the 3D reference.
4. Photograph the gameboy on set.
5. Retouch.

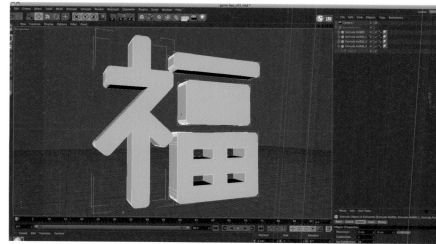

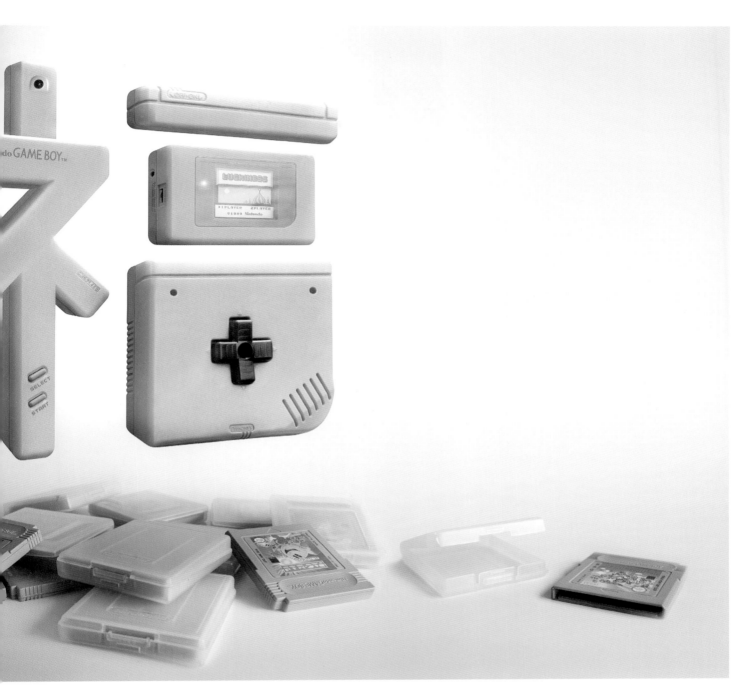

Meadowhall 25 Years

Designer   Kyle Wilkinson   *Client*   Meadowhall Centre
Design Agency   Hacksaw™ Studio

Meadowhall Centre welcomes over 26 million visitors a year and is one of the UK's largest shopping malls. To celebrate their 25th birthday they came to Hacksaw™ for a bold and fun campaign that injected a splash of color throughout the Mall. The solution was a Carnival style celebration with a hand made, paper cut illustration that was used alongside a variety of Carnival themed live acts.

Materials & tools

paper, colored paper, pen, scalpel, tweezers, scissors

Process

1. Draw the initial sketch of the Meadowhall campaign.

2. Begin the paper cut process, the whole piece was cut by hand with a scalpel.

3. Add paper layers to give depth to the typography and give a 3D feel to the whole piece.

4. Put all the elements together to build the paper cut set.

		3
1	2	4

Good Enough

Design Agency   Autobahn
Client   Volkskrant Magazine

Photographer   Daan Paans

This is a typographic illustration in the Dutch Volkskrant Magazine that accompanied the article on the new book 'The Heart of All Things' by Elizabeth Gilbert (known for Eat, Pray, Love) which addresses a botanical theme. The illustrations were made by hand using 'original orange' pottery clay and small plants.

1a	1b	2a	2b
1c		3	

Materials & tools

pottery clay, camera, Photoshop

Process

1. Buy terracotta clay and shape the letterforms.

2. Buy plants and garden soil then put everything in the letterforms.

3. Space the letters correctly and photograph them.

Laie String Type

Designer   Brandon T. Truscott
Client   BYU – Hawaii

The Laie sign string typography was created to commemorate the 60th anniversary of BYU – Hawaii in Laie, Hawaii. The sign was purchased by the university and is now on permanent display at the Polynesian Cultural Center.

1	2
3	

Materials & tools

plywood, nails, string

Process

1. The sign was designed in Adobe Illustrator using vector paths and dotted lines and traced onto a 48 inch painted black square plywood board.

2. Nails were pounded into the plywood board.

3. String was woven around the nails.

(Video of production: https://vimeo.com/brandontruscott/laiestringtype)

La Pegatina

Designer Noelia Lozano
Client   La Pegatina

This year the Spanish rumba fusion band "La Pegatina" are celebrating their 10th anniversary. The designer was commissioned to create a logo on paper for one of the t-shirts for their anniversary.

Materials & tools

paper, scissors, glue, scalpel, ruler, color papers, foam, cutting base

Process

1. Create your sketch for your illustration. Divide by color and print on different paper colors.

2. Start cutting the different parts of the illustrations.

3. Save all the tiny parts and organize carefully by color.

4. Cut the different parts.

5. Put all the parts together to create the layers of the logo.

6. Finish by putting color drops and details around the logo.

7. Create a nice lighting set and take the final picture of the logo. Retouch the final image.

1	2
3	4
5	6
	7

Chalkboard Lettering

Designer Scott Biersack

In this day and age, especially with the economy the way it is, times are tough. With that, the designer used his skill set to instill motivation and inspiration in people's days by writing some motivational quotes and phrases on a public 8ft tall by 15ft wide chalkboard. He drew a new motivational piece on that board every Saturday for almost an entire year to brighten up the days of those that might be struggling, and to spread these positive messages to make it a better day.

Materials & tools

chalk

#Wayofplay

Design Agency   Autobahn
Client   Sony Playstation Network

To visualize the #Wayofplay, or commands of Playstation Network users for a European campaign, Autobahn has designed a typeface. The typeface comes in two versions: a highlight side and a shadow side of stone carved letters. Designers can use the two versions in any design program and make it look like the text is carved in stone.

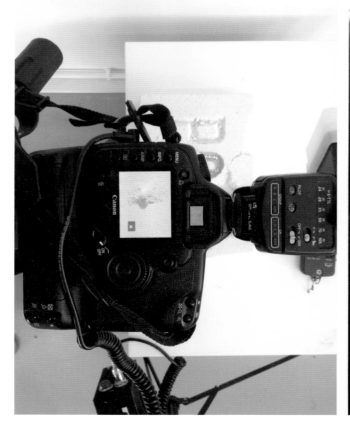

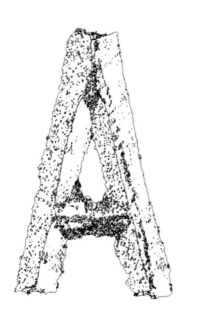
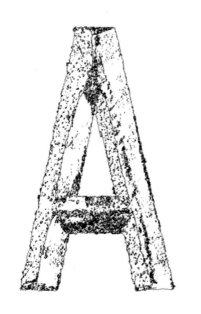
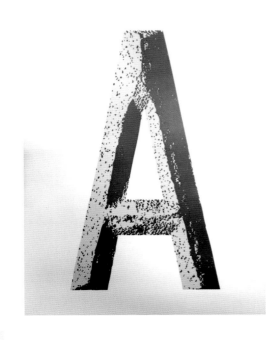

!"#%'()*+,-./:;=?@\^`-¨´

0123456789

ABCDEFGHIJKLM
NOPQRSTUVWXYZ

ABCDEFGHIJKLM
NOPQRSTUVWXYZ

ÀÁÂÃÄÅÆÇÈÉÊËÌÍÎÏÑ
ÒÓÔÕÖØÙÚÛÜÝŸ

ÀÁÂÃÄÅÆÇÈÉÊËÌÍÎÏ
ÒÓÔÕÖØÙÚÛÜÝÑß

ŒŒŠŠŸŽŽ ˚ '''¦¦¦

1	2	5	6
3	4		7

Materials & tools

concrete, hammer, chisel, camera, Photoshop, Illustrator

Process

1. Trace the letterforms you want to cut on a slab of stone (in this case concrete).

2. Use a hammer and chisel to cut the left and right side of the letters towards the center.

3. Photograph every letter individually.

4. Adjust the rotation and size in Photoshop, and cut the letters from the background.

5. Trace the letters in Illustrator.

6. Define the shadow side by making it black and define the highlight side by making it grey.

7. Separate the highlight from the shadow side and overlay the two to adjust the effect manually.

Forever Alone — Anti-Valentine's Card

Lettering & Designer	Jess Caddick		*Photographer*	Ed Fury
Production	Jess Caddick, Craig Gittins		*Design Agency*	Green Chameleon

The Green Chameleon 'Anti-Valentine's Card' was created in retaliation to the corny expectations developed from the evolution of Saint Valentine's Day in a modern western society. The approach toward the self-initiated project is pure sugar-coated irony, and some of the merchandise flogged on the day are used to misdirect the viewer on the intention of the message.

Materials & tools

sweets, chocolates, flowers, pink backdrop, brush

Process

1. Smashed sweets into crumbs, placed them onto a custom stencil on a blank canvas.

2. Carefully brushed the sweets into place, allowing some areas to have more depth.

3. Collected Valentine's materials and placed around the edges of the artwork for effect.

4. Photographed for post-production. Used Photoshop to enhance the final design by removing any unwanted elements and making some final placement adjustments.

1	2	3b
3a		4

Merry Christmas Card

Lettering & Designer Jess Caddick
Production Nathan Riley, Jess Caddick, Craig Gittins, Nathan Riley, Tom Anderson

Photographer Ed Fury
Design Agency Green Chameleon

The Christmas card was created from of a collection of festive materials, then photographed, printed and sent out to Green Chameleon's family, friends and colleagues in 2015. The focus of the artwork was to use only Christmas elements to create something that was visually impactful, triggering a sense of sentiment and nostalgia.

		3	
1	2	4a	4b

Materials & tools

Christmas tree pines, shortbread biscuits, fake snow, Christmas items, slate backdrop, brush, cutting knife

Process

1. A stencil was created from the design and used as guideline for the lettering.

2. Brushes and knives were used to push tree pines and biscuit crumbs into place.

3. The edges were scattered with festive items for balance and composition.

4. The finished piece was photographed, and the levels adjusted in Photoshop to make it pop!

Candy is Dandy

Art Director	Nathan Riley
Lettering	Jess Caddick
Client	Don't Panic

Production	Nathan Riley, Jess Caddick, Craig Gittins
Design Agency	Green Chameleon

To commemorate the 50th anniversary of Roald Dahl's deliciously dark novel 'Charlie and The Chocolate Factory', Don't Panic teamed up with Sam Mendes' gigantic new stage musical to call for a nostalgic poster to celebrate the milestone. Green Chameleon used the brief as a guideline and focused on creating this food typography piece 'Candy is Dandy.' The poster was handcrafted entirely from sweets and is completely edible.

Materials & tools

candies, strawberry laces, chocolate, sherbet, glue, cutting knife, brush

Process

1. Collected a variety of candies to create the lettering.

2. Because the candies are tricky to position, glue was used to keep the design in place.

3. For the strawberry laces, a cutting knife was required for precision.

4. A brush was used to clean away unwanted candies before the piece was photographed.

Bufona, Something Like a Typeface

Designer Javier Jaén

This personal project "Bufona, something like a typeface" is inspired by "Everything is amazing and nobody is happy," a quote by Louis CK. To execute the production, the designer used balloons of different colors, and more than 150 handmade balloon characters are the final results.

BUFONA

A A B B C C Ç D D E E
F F G G H H I I J J K K
L L M M N N Ñ Ñ O O P P
Q Q R R S S T T U U V V
W W X X Y Y Z Z

0 0 1 1 2 2 3 3 4 4 5 5
6 6 7 7 8 8 9 9

Ä Ä Â Â Á Á À À
Ë Ë Ê Ê É É È È
Ï Ï Î Î Í Í Ì Ì
Ö Ö Ô Ô Ó Ó Ò Ò
Ü Ü Û Û Ú Ú Ù Ù
¿ ¿ ? ? € € £ £

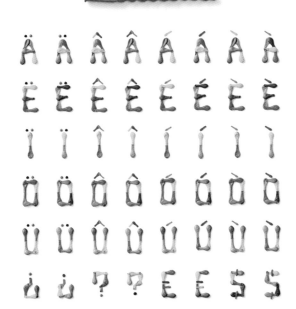

4	3
1 2	

Materials & tools

balloons, glue

Process

1. To reproduce the Bufona typeface, fold and combine the balloons.

2. Glue the letters and let them dry.

3. Reproduce the entire alphabet with all letters, numbers and special characters.

4. Once it is complete, duplicate the entire set to avoid repetition in shapes and colors.

Index

Acknowledgements

We would like to thank all the designers and contributors who have been involved in the production of this book; their contributions have been indispensable to its creation. We would also like to express our gratitude to all the producers for their invaluable opinions and assistance throughout this project. And to the many others whose names are not credited but have made helpful suggestions, we thank you for your continuous support.

Future Cooperations

If you wish to participate in SendPoints' future projects and publications, please send your website or portfolio to editor01@sendpoints.cn.